*Salvation Through*
# JUDGMENT
AND
# MERCY

THE GOSPEL ACCORDING TO
THE OLD TESTAMENT

A series of studies on the lives
of Old Testament characters, written for
laypeople and pastors, and designed to
encourage Christ-centered reading, teaching,
and preaching of the Old Testament.

TREMPER LONGMAN III
J. ALAN GROVES

*Series Editors*

*After God's Own Heart,* by Mark J. Boda
*Crying Out for Vindication,* by David R. Jackson
*Faith in the Face of Apostasy,* by Raymond B. Dillard
*From Famine to Fullness,* by Dean R. Ulrich
*Hope in the Midst of a Hostile World,* by George M.
  Schwab
*Immanuel In Our Place,* by Tremper Longman III
*Living in the Gap Between Promise and Reality,* by
  Iain M. Duguid
*Living in the Grip of Relentless Grace,* by Iain M. Duguid
*Love Divine and Unfailing,* by Michael P. V. Barrett
*Salvation Through Judgment and Mercy,* by
  Bryan D. Estelle
*Longing for God in an Age of Discouragement,* by
  Bryan R. Gregory
*Right in Their Own Eyes,* by George M. Schwab

# Salvation Through
# JUDGMENT
## AND
# MERCY

### THE GOSPEL ACCORDING TO
## JONAH

## BRYAN D. ESTELLE

P U B L I S H I N G

P.O. BOX 817 • PHILLIPSBURG • NEW JERSEY 08865-0817

*Page design by Tobias Design*

*Typesetting by Lakeside Design Plus*

Printed in the United States of America

**Library of Congress Cataloging-in-Publication Data**

Estelle, Bryan D., 1959–
       Salvation through judgment and mercy : the Gospel according
to Jonah / Bryan D. Estelle.
               p. cm. — (The Gospel according to the Old Testament)
       Includes bibliographical references (p. ) and index.
       ISBN-13: 978-0-87552-656-0 (pbk.)
       ISBN-10: 0-87552-656-X (pbk.)
       1. Salvation. 2. Bible. O.T. Jonah—Criticism, interpretation, etc.
       I. Title. II. Series.

BS1605.6.S25E88  2005
224'.9206—dc22

                                                        2005047403

# CONTENTS

# FOREWORD

*The New Testament is in the Old concealed;*
*the Old Testament is in the New revealed.*
*—Augustine*

Concerning this salvation, the prophets, who spoke of
the grace that was to come to you, searched intently
and with the greatest care, trying to find out the time
and circumstances to which the Spirit of Christ in them
was pointing when he predicted the sufferings of Christ
and the glories that would follow. It was revealed to
them that they were not serving themselves but you,
when they spoke of the things that have now been told
you by those who have preached the gospel to you by
the Holy Spirit sent from heaven. Even angels long to
look into these things. (1 Peter 1:10–12)

"In addition, some of our women amazed us. They
went to the tomb early this morning but didn't find his
body. They came and told us that they had seen a
vision of angels, who said he was alive. Then some of
our companions went to the tomb and found it just as
the women had said, but him they did not see." He said
to them, "How foolish you are, and how slow of heart
to believe all that the prophets have spoken! Did not
the Christ have to suffer these things and then enter his
glory?" And beginning with Moses and all the Prophets,
he explained to them what was said in all the Scriptures
concerning himself. (Luke 24:22–27)

The prophets searched. Angels longed to see. And the disciples didn't understand. But Moses, the prophets, and all the Old Testament Scriptures had spoken about it—that Jesus would come, suffer, and then be glorified. God began to tell a story in the Old Testament, the ending of which the audience eagerly anticipated. But the Old Testament audience was left hanging. The plot was laid out but the climax was delayed. The unfinished story begged an ending. In Christ, God has provided the climax to the Old Testament story. Jesus did not arrive unannounced; his coming was declared *in advance* in the Old Testament, not just in explicit prophecies of the Messiah but by means of the stories of all of the events, characters, and circumstances in the Old Testament. God was telling a larger, overarching, unified story. From the account of creation in Genesis to the final stories of the return from exile, God progressively unfolded his plan of salvation. And the Old Testament account of that plan always pointed in some way to Christ.

## AIMS OF THIS SERIES

The Gospel According to the Old Testament Series is committed to the proposition that the Bible, both Old and New Testaments, is a unified revelation of God, and that its thematic unity is found in Christ. The individual books of the Old Testament exhibit diverse genres, styles, and individual theologies, but tying them all together is the constant foreshadowing of, and pointing forward to, Christ. Believing in the fundamentally Christocentric nature of the Old Testament, as well as the New Testament, we offer this series of studies in the Old Testament with the following aims:

- to lay out the pervasiveness of the revelation of Christ in the Old Testament

- to promote a Christ-centered reading of the Old Testament
- to encourage Christ-centered preaching and teaching from the Old Testament

To these ends, the volumes in this series are written for pastors and laypeople, not scholars.

While such a series could take a number of different shapes, we have decided, in most cases, to focus individual volumes on Old Testament figures—people—rather than books or themes. Some books, of course, will receive major attention in connection with their authors or main characters (e.g., Daniel or Isaiah). Also, certain themes will be emphasized in connection with particular figures.

It is our hope and prayer that this series will revive interest in and study of the Old Testament as readers recognize that the Old Testament points forward to Jesus Christ.

TREMPER LONGMAN III
J. ALAN GROVES

# ACKNOWLEDGMENTS

It is now my pleasure and joy to thank many who have helped me on this project. I am well aware that this book has been a cooperative work. I am grateful to my colleagues at Westminster Seminary in California and the board of trustees for granting me a sabbatical in the fall of 2004. Much of the writing of this book took place during that time.

A number of people read part or all of this manuscript. Tremper Longman III was not only a helpful editor throughout the process, but he matched my diffidence with unexpected encouragement. My wife Lisa read the introductory chapter and asked a number of good questions that sent me back to the computer in order to strive for clarity. Without her, and the encouragement of my children, Sean, David, and Kaitlin, this project never would have seen the light of day.

Several colleagues at the seminary, Iain Duguid, Julius Kim, and David VanDrunen, read portions of the manuscript and made helpful suggestions. James Lund (our steadfast librarian) and his assistant Judith Riddell kept interlibrary loan books and articles coming on this project and many others. One of my students, Brent England, read the entire manuscript and saved me from a number of errors.

I must thank the editors of P&R Publishing for their thorough reading of this work. I am indebted to them for a number of excellent suggestions on style.

Kelli Garvey, a member of Knox Orthodox Presbyterian Church, was a tenacious reader, editor, and friend throughout the process of writing. Her support was representative of the broader clan at Knox OPC. I would also like to thank a graduate student at Westminster Seminary, Clayton Willis, for his assistance with computer-related problems. On this project, and others as well, I want to acknowledge my indebtedness.

This, my first book, is dedicated to a man who throughout my life has demonstrably echoed God's character to me. To my father, Walter Estelle, I dedicate this labor.

# INTRODUCTION

Shipmates, this book containing only four chapters—four yarns—is one of the smallest strands in the mighty cable of the Scriptures. Yet what depths of the soul does Jonah's deep sealine sound! What a pregnant lesson to us is this prophet! What a noble thing is that canticle in the fish's belly! How billow-like and boisterously grand! (Herman Melville, *Moby Dick*)

You diligently study the Scriptures because you think that by them you possess eternal life. These are the Scriptures that testify about me. (John 5:39)

In spite of its brevity, the book of Jonah is not easy to interpret. Although the story is clear and simple enough for a child to grasp, a feature that helps to explain its popularity in the Sunday school curriculum and vacation Bible schools throughout the world, a personal letter by Augustine of Hippo sums up well the difficulties contained in this little book: "What he asks about the resurrection of the dead could be settled. . . . But if he thinks to solve all such questions as . . . those about Jonah . . . he little knows the limitations of human life or his own."[1]

Reading the book in Hebrew (something at which Augustine, in spite of his brilliance, did not excel) will not serve to simplify the difficulties because the book's artistry is complex and richly displayed. Below the surface simplicity of this biblical book, the prophecy of Jonah is an extremely subtle and complex piece of work. I continue to bump up against the reality that easy answers are not forthcoming; rather, the original author, a very thoughtful and skilled author indeed, kept questions alive for his audience. Therefore, we should not reduce this story to one simple theological message. The story of Jonah, in fact, evokes questions that will probably not find answers even after repeatedly rereading the book.

This is often what makes a classic: wonderful literary artistry mixed with many layers of meaning that motivate reading a book more than just once. Consequently, a person ought to read a classic thoughtfully, slowly, and repeatedly. A classic endures the test of time. The book of Jonah is a classic.

Reading Jonah is like standing before a great mountain. Having trained hard and being well prepared for the climb, one might assume that a successful ascent (as well as the descent) is assured. Such an attitude, as every experienced mountain climber knows, is foolhardy. And like great mountains, great books command respect. The poet William Blake said that great things happen when men and mountains meet; how much more so when people with the right orientation encounter great books.

There are numerous books and commentaries on Jonah readily available, so why write another? I believe there is room for another book on Jonah, specifically a book that fits into the aims of this series. What is necessary for today are commentaries and books that responsibly present the biblical writings in their canonical context. The present need in the church is for books that promote responsible Christ-centered reading, preaching, and teaching of the Old Testament. E. J. Young recognized years ago that the main message of Jonah is focused on Christ: "The fundamental purpose of the book of Jonah is not found in its missionary or universalistic teaching. It is rather to show that Jonah being cast into the depths of Sheol and yet brought up alive is an illustration of the death of the Messiah for sins not His own and of the Messiah's resurrection."[2]

In spite of all the difficulties alluded to previously, we must give the book of Jonah a Christian reading. Jonah, first and foremost, plain and simple, has this most important message for the Christian church today: *Christ, the risen One who is greater than Jonah, brings salvation through judgment and mercy to his people, those inside and outside of Israel who call on his name.* What is foreshadowed and illustrated in Jonah becomes reality in Christ.

Acknowledging this up front gives recognition to one of the most fundamental points of theological method. Indeed, since Christ is the focal event of all salvation history and since we read the books of the Bible following that climactic event, we must read Jonah through Christocentric glasses. After surveying in great detail Jesus' own use of the Old Testament, R. T. France summed this up well: "Jesus understood the Old Testament Christologically: in its essential principles, and even in its details, it foreshadows the Messiah whom it promises. The whole theological system of the Old Testament points forward to his work, and in his coming the whole Old Testament economy finds its perfection and fulfillment."[3] This conclusion does not deny the fact that the Old Testament is theocentric (God-centered); it merely points the spotlight exactly where the thrice-holy God was delighted to place it: on Christ.

Notice also the phraseology above: "salvation through judgment and mercy." As the great Princeton theologian Charles Hodge has said, it is important not to merge justice into benevolence. Other Reformed theologians have emphasized the importance of not representing mercy to the neglect of justice. This is especially important in our own culture because there is such a strong trend to suppress the concepts of divine judgment and justice to the point that mercy and compassion become watered down into nothing more than sentimentality. Both themes, judgment and mercy, must be held forth.

With regard to mercy, we will note the mercy of Israel's God as evidenced by his treatment of so many characters in the book of Jonah: the sailors, Jonah himself, the Ninevites, and the animals as well! By saying that this is a central message I do not mean to oversimplify the book. Indeed, it is premature to state what the central message of the book is without plowing through the details of the book first. The reader will have that opportunity in the pages that follow.

In fact, much more will be said in the following chapters to unpack this general theme of the Christocentric (Christ-centered) nature of Jonah. Although I affirm that the Old Testament is Christocentric, that does not mean that every Christocentric reading of an Old Testament text is a legitimate one. There have been times in the history of the church (and the practice has not completely passed away) when Christ-centered readings of Old Testament texts have run amuck. Some preachers and teachers are too quick to make the typological jump from the Old Testament without responsibly informing their audiences how they got there.

Jerome (an early Latin church father, born about 347 A.D.), for example, suggested that "Jonah is like Christ because Christ fled the heavens to come to Tarshish, that is, 'the sea of this world,' and Jonah in flight is a sign of the incarnate Christ, who 'abandons his father's house and country, and becomes flesh.'"[4] Augustine interpreted the worm that devours the plant in chapter 4 as Christ, since in him the privileges of the Old Covenant are devoured. Despite such unfettered imaginative freedom, it does not follow that we should be bashful about observing the pervasiveness of Christ in the book of Jonah or in other Old Testament books.

Some very modern commentators warn against the Christian colonization of the book of Jonah. Such a warning, it seems to me, is enslaved to the discourse of power structures (a very modern manner of interpretation) when it comes to reading texts rather than being truly in touch with the pulse of Scripture. It is true that we must take care not to foist an unwarranted understanding upon the text of Scripture. Nevertheless, what is needed is a thoughtful approach toward a Christocentric understanding of the book of Jonah.

With this goal in mind, Scripture must be understood as an organic unity. The Hebrew Bible is not a self-contained unit, for there is the expectation of fulfillment throughout. This truth necessitates that one will find the ultimate meaning of the Old Testament, that is, the Hebrew Scriptures, in the New Testament. More precisely, the interpretation of any given particular text must be considered in the light of its canonical context within Scripture itself. This is not the first step in understanding a text, but it is a necessary step. Nor is this approach to be practiced in such a way that it does injury to the individual character of books of the Old Testament. With this caveat in mind, the following pages will situate the book of Jonah in its canonical context and examine its Christocentric focus. Discovering Christ in the Old Testament literature takes work and is not easy. Applications must be made slowly and carefully. In short, such an approach must not be overly facile.

A few more introductory comments will aid the reader. The book is written first and foremost for pastors and laypeople, not for the guild of professional biblical scholars. Therefore, although the reader will notice in places that I have presented different possible interpretations, in the main I have taken pains not to obscure the text by evaluating every competing opinion on the passage under consideration. I have written with pastors especially in mind since this is the aim of this series, and since I have received many requests from our knights in the pulpit for help on this little book. But this book was written also with laypeople in mind. This aim is equally important. Some parts will probably stretch certain readers because of their difficulty. I am a great believer in education, however, and hope that any exertion on the reader's part because I've not been clear enough will reap multiple dividends in the end. For example, chapter 1 has some important historical background to the book of Jonah. I've tried not to make it too cumbersome. If the reader will work through it, the rest of the book will probably make more sense.

I have included—unobtrusively, I trust—some comments about the Hebrew text so that the reader may have a greater appreciation for the beauty and meaning of this little masterpiece, the book of Jonah. Just as I desire to help my Hebrew students see in color as well as black and white when exposing them to the beauties of reading Scripture in the original language, I hope to do something similar for the general reader of this book. In other words, by including some simple comments about the Hebrew, I want to help the reader both smell the rose and see it, so to speak.

All dates for kings and rulers, whether inside or outside Israel, are taken from the excellent two-volume history of the ancient Near East by Amélie Kuhrt. I have also given a number of Scripture references where this is appropriate. Often when I am reading a book with Scripture references, I will pause in my reading and take time to look up those references in order to appreciate the point the author wishes to make. Generally I have found such a practice to be instructive and edifying. The Scripture references peppered throughout this book are given for similar reasons. The reader would do well to keep a Bible in hand.

Taking my cue from the Italian poet Vittorio Imbriani who quipped, "Traduttore, traditore," which roughly translated means something like "Every translator a traitor," I have left a few words from the Hebrew text of Jonah in simple transliteration because they defy translation. That is to say, something is always lost in translation. For example, the plant that quickly grows up over Jonah's head to provide shade for him is called a *qiqayon*. Commentators debate back and forth as to what this plant was or could have possibly been. In fact (if one can imagine it!), emotions ran so high concerning the translation of this word that a riot almost broke out in Augustine's day over translation preferences. I simply signal the transliteration to the reader when the word first appears, explain why I am choosing to leave it in transliteration, and then proceed to use the Hebrew word in the remainder of the book. The reader having been warned beforehand will have no difficulty following along. I have chosen this practice for only a few words that the reader will encounter in the book of Jonah.

# I

## ORIENTATION

Heaven have mercy on us all—Presbyterians and
Pagans alike—for we are all somehow dreadfully
cracked about the head, and sadly need mending.
(Herman Melville, *Moby Dick*)

The word of the LORD came to Jonah son of Amittai . . .
(Jonah 1:1)

### DATE AND COMPOSITION

Modern men and women often possess an arrogant attitude toward the people who have gone before them. This
is especially the case with respect to antiquity. C. S. Lewis
called this the chronological fallacy: a mode of thinking
that is dismissive of ideas simply because they are not new.
Ancient men and women, it is alleged, had no capacity for
abstraction and metaphor and must have been simpletons
accepting everything in a literalistic manner. Doubtless, it
is assumed by many as well that the ancients had no facil-
ity for beauty, aesthetics, or superior taste. Such notions
betray an arrogance that is pitiable in many modern minds.

We live in an age that often does not appreciate the past and the lessons to be learned there. That requires sitting still for long periods of reading, not something in which our culture is very proficient. Our hectic velocity of life drives us to search the Internet for information while gaining only a superficial knowledge about many things, but is this natural? Studying the past, let alone the art of writing about past events, requires slow and careful reading and is essential to a proper understanding of the Bible.

This very common modern neglect impoverishes our cultural lives, and when it spills over into our reading of the Bible, it will impoverish our appreciation of the riches of Scripture as well. Understanding the Bible correctly entails that we exert a little effort to understand the past, even a very ancient past.

For its mere forty-eight verses, the book of Jonah has attracted a stunning amount of attention from the scholarly community. Yet, despite all the discussion, very little consensus exists on introductory matters such as when Jonah was written. Dating a biblical book, if one is confidently able to do so, is important because dating could alter the interpretation of the book's contents.

From the perspective of the book of Jonah as it comes to us, the events related are portrayed as occurring in the eighth century B.C. In other words, this is the historical context in which the author wished to portray the events he describes. The biblical narrative here is often very selective, artistically arranged, and didactic. In other words, it is not merely a journalistic reporting of events; on the contrary, the narrative is describing and interpreting the events that are being reported. It is typical in this day to pit historical narration over and against artistic literary arrangement. Consider, for example, the following questions asked by one recent commentator on Jonah: "Is it [i.e., Jonah] a prophetic story like those of Elijah, clearly intending to narrate actual facts? Or is it a fictional tale like that of Job, intended to express theological verities in artistic language?"[1] Many commentators recognize that Jonah has similarities with the records of Elijah and Elisha. Even so, this kind of statement is problematic at a number of levels that space limitations do not allow me to discuss at the present time. However, at least one thing this statement seems to be doing (among others) is placing the issues of historical narration and artistic representation on the horns of an unnecessary dilemma. This is wrong, as we will see later.

We know the author wished to portray the events as occurring in the eighth century B.C. because of the very first verse, which alludes to "Jonah ben Amittai" (Jonah the son of Amittai). According to 2 Kings 14:25, the prophetic words of Jonah son of Amittai were fulfilled during the reign of King Jeroboam II (786–746 B.C.). Of course this does not prove that the prophet and the king were immediate contemporaries. Nor does it prove that Jonah himself wrote the book of Jonah (*contra* E. J. Young). Nowhere does the book declare that Jonah wrote it. What can we say confidently, then, about the book's composition?

While the book has been dated as early as the eighth century, it definitely cannot be dated any later than the third century B.C. because it is mentioned in an apocryphal work entitled Ben Sira, usually dated to approximately 180 B.C. Attempts at reaching a firm conclusion about both the date and the composition of this little prophetical book are made more difficult by many other complex issues: our present knowledge of ancient languages, the genre to which the book belongs, historical awareness of the ancient world, and pinpointing the book's specific audience. If language alone were the sole criterion, then the book was probably composed during a late period, since the stage of Hebrew represented is most likely very late according to our current understanding of the development of Hebrew. However, dating books on linguistic criteria alone is a risky endeavor, and the results of such studies are often debatable for a number of other reasons. In short, beyond the portrayal by the author (i.e., the events described occur during the eighth century B.C.), the book of Jonah does not assign a specific date or author to its composition.

So then, dating the composition of the book should not be an orthodox litmus test for a preacher or teacher of this masterful short story. The didactic message of this sacred history—a history which is also selective, artistic, and covenantal—communicates effectively and accurately despite the differences of opinion with respect to dating, authorship, and composition. Even so, a bird's-eye perspective of Israel's situation in the unfolding developments of God's plan for his people at the time represented in the biblical story may provide a very important interpretative grid through which a reader may understand the book of Jonah.

Although the author situates the book against a broad historical backdrop, some scholars have attempted to suggest a more precise date for the composition of the book of Jonah based on the probable presence of questions of theodicy.[2] Theodicy is literally the "justification of God." Often the term arises in theological and philosophical discussions when the problem of evil and suffering is under consideration. Specifically, some scholars suggest possible dates for Jonah as sometime following the fall of the capital of the Northern Kingdom (i.e., 722 B.C.) when questions of theodicy probably surfaced. The remaining Israelites may have asked themselves if all this suffering could really be part of God's sovereign plan. Could Israel's own covenant God allow Assyria (Israel's enemy) to do this to God's chosen people?

While this is a possible scenario, the fact of the matter is that God's people have dealt with, and will have to wrestle with, questions of theodicy in every age. Suffering is part and parcel of the existence of God's pilgrim people in this life. Furthermore, a precise date of composition is not crucial for our understanding of the book, nor does predicating an "early" date give further weight to the historical veracity of the material reported in the book. In the final analysis, the date of composition, although possibly enhancing our understanding of the book, does not matter a great deal to the ultimate theological message or the issue of the historicity of the book of Jonah. If that were the case, then "much of that which we read in our history books would rest on shaky ground indeed."[3]

Although these and other issues could be discussed in great detail, it is quite outside the aims of this series to do so (see the foreword by Tremper Longman and Alan Groves). Instead, broader features of the setting as portrayed by the author of the book of Jonah can and should be discussed.

First, the way in which Jonah is introduced in the Hebrew text indicates that the prophet was a figure who was already known to the audience or at least had been mentioned previously. In other words, Jonah is an established figure given the manner in which he is introduced in Hebrew idiom. This is an insuperable fact with which commentators wrestle in various ways.

Second, an appreciation of what Assyria (and hence Nineveh, the great city of the Assyrians) meant to Israel may help the reader understand the book of Jonah better. If we assume that the perspective of the book is the eighth century B.C., then Assyria probably had been, or currently was, and more than likely soon would be a threat against Israel. Since the book is portrayed from the perspective of the time when Jonah the son of Amittai mentioned in 2 Kings was probably active (in the reign of Jeroboam II, i.e., 786–746 B.C.), it is important to note that Assyria had already exacted tribute from another earlier Israelite king named Jehu (842–815 B.C.). In fact, Jeroboam II was the fourth king in Jehu's dynasty.

Jehu, a king of Israel, eradicated (at least outwardly) Baal worship from Israel (see especially 2 Kings 9 and 10). Because of this work, God said he would reward Jehu's dynasty for four generations (i.e., down to Jeroboam II; 2 Kings 10:30). King Jehu is represented on the famous Black Obelisk of Shalmaneser III (858–824 B.C.) from Kalhu. This Assyrian obelisk is well preserved and may be seen at the British Museum in London (copies may be seen in some American universities as well). The obelisk serves as a symbol of Assyrian expansionistic policies shortly before the time in which Jonah prophesied. At one place on the obelisk the subjugation of Jehu is depicted. The obelisk reads in the Akkadian language, "I [Shalmaneser] received the tribute of the inhabitants of Tyre, Sidon, and of Jehu, son of Omri."[4] The crucial point is this: Assyria as a threatening neighboring superpower during the eighth century B.C. was probably still a recent and ominous memory in the collective conscience of the Israelites.

Furthermore, even though Assyria's former power and glory had receded temporarily at the time of Jeroboam II's reign, the time at which some of Jonah's prophecies were fulfilled, the Assyrian superpower was soon to return to and even exceed its former position of power and expansion. The prophecies of Hosea and Amos, for example, predicted imminent disaster at the hands of the Assyrians. In fact, in 743 B.C. and the following years, when Tiglath-pileser III (744–727 B.C.) and his sons Shalmaneser V (726–722) and Sargon II (721–705) reigned, there would be a reassertion of Assyrian power against neighbors to the west (e.g., Israel). As is well known, the Northern Kingdom of Israel and its capital Samaria were destined to fall to the mighty Assyrians in 722 B.C. It is well nigh impossible, therefore, to imagine that any Israelite during or after this time—including a period when Assyria receded from expansionistic policies to shore up her strongholds—would have had a neutral emotional reaction when the name of Assyria was mentioned.

## THE DISTINCTIVENESS OF ISRAEL
## AND COVENANT INFIDELITY

Although a specific date of composition cannot be assigned to the book of Jonah, we can determine a broader historical view from the perspective of the book as we have received it. The little book of Jonah forces the reader right at the beginning to ask the question, "Why is Jonah, a prophet of God, called to go to a Gentile nation, when the mission of most of the prophets of Israel and Judah (though not exclusively) is to prophesy to or against God's chosen people, that is, Israel and Judah?" In other words, "Why is Jonah commissioned to go to a foreign nation rather than to his own people?" Furthermore, "What is the relationship between Israel and the nations at this time in history?"

Many have tried to respond to these questions by asserting a kind of universalism (defined as communicating God's compassion for the nations outside of Israel) that pervades the book of Jonah. This answer, however, as pointed out many years ago by Edmund Clowney, is only superficially satisfying.[5]

We need to stand back and distinguish the forest from the trees before we begin looking at the details of the book. We need to ask what the big picture was with respect to God's interactions with the people of Israel at that time in history. By doing so, we are not in danger of reading a message into Jonah that is not there; on the contrary, we are recognizing that discerning a broad context can help us understand the particulars and details of the book. Also, we are sensitizing ourselves to the particular period of redemptive history in which the contents of this book are portrayed. This is one of the first and necessary important steps in the process of interpretation.

Let the reader understand that this is a different issue than determining exactly who the intended audience is. Since the exact date of composition is unknown, the answer to that question is that the intended audience is simply God's people in each successive generation. The book of Jonah was intended for God's people in ancient Israel, and it was intended for God's people after Christ came. Even so, we are about to embark on another important preliminary task: we are going to determine in broad strokes what God's relationships with his people and with the Gentiles were during the period in which the author has placed the events described.

God's relationship with his chosen people is the lens through which one may understand the history of Israel correctly. To state it simply, the essence of God's relationship with his people can be summed up in a word: covenant. A covenant may be broadly defined as a commitment with divine sanctions.[6] Biblical covenants often have solemn oaths attached to them. God promises to be the God of Israel, and the Israelites promise to be exclusively his people.

Jonah's commission in chapter 1 must be understood against the backdrop of the Mosaic covenant. However, the Mosaic covenant must in turn be understood against the backdrop of the patriarchs, particularly the covenant with Abraham. In what is often alluded to by theologians as the covenant of grace, God promised that all the peoples on the earth would be blessed through Abraham's seed (Gen. 12:1–3; 18:18; 22:18). Here is eschatology already present in God's dealings with his people. That is, it is forward-looking. Clowney states this felicitously:

> Even in the Abrahamic period of revelation there comes, along with the development of particularism

of grace, a revelation that in Abraham's seed all the nations of the earth will be blessed. The setting up of the seed of Abraham is a particularistic means to a universal end of blessing. Even in this period it is to be noted that this blessing has an eschatological position. It is connected with the seed (Gen. 17:7), which, as Paul reminds us, is not the many, but the one, that coming One whose day Abraham saw and was glad (Gal. 3:16).[7]

Some recent commentators on the book of Jonah have stated that "explicit references to the covenant theme are noticeably absent from Jonah."[8] If we were to accent the term "explicit," then that statement could be considered true enough. Nevertheless, that there are no explicit references to covenant does not mean that the concept of covenant is absent from the book. The Israelites were a covenantal people. Let me explain.

Covenant is an essential background belief for the book of Jonah. God's covenantal dealings with the Israelites are taken for granted. When doing biblical studies, one needs to discriminate between the term and the idea behind it. Even without an explicit reference we can still assume a historical covenant. This touches on an axiom (i.e., a principle that doesn't need to be proven) of both theology and linguistics: a term or word does not have to be present in order for the concept to be present. As a New Testament colleague of mine is fond of saying, "If it quacks like a duck, then it is a duck." In short, the book of Jonah assumes God's dealings with Israel through covenant; this concept was so pervasive to the Israelites that it didn't need to be explicitly mentioned.

Thus the backdrop of God's covenant dealings with Israel is assumed in the book of Jonah. The idea lay in back of the words of the book of Jonah even though the exact word for "covenant" (*berit*) is not present in the book; indeed, it may be correctly asserted, as Peter Craigie did in fact assert, that Jonah "had a strongly-based covenant theology."[9]

This is a crucial step in the process of interpreting biblical books correctly: knowledge of both the historical background and the covenantal context will often enhance our understanding of a particular text. A couple of historical examples will serve as an illustration. An awareness of the availability of iron in Israel or lack thereof might explain the great anxiety and distress experienced by an Israelite losing a borrowed axe (2 Kings 6:1–7). Or, for example, the interpretation of the language and book of Esther is illuminated by familiarity with the history of ancient Persia.

It is true that the book of Jonah doesn't begin with the same kind of specific and detailed historical references that many of the other prophetical books do (e.g., Jer. 1:1–3; Ezek. 1:2; Hos. 1:1; Amos 1:1). Caution is warranted when searching for historical connections, especially if one has a theological axe to grind. However, I would suggest that an acquaintance with the general historical period in which the story is couched is crucial to a correct understanding and interpretation of the story.

The author has taken pains to connect our Jonah with the Jonah alluded to in 2 Kings 14 by the way he opens his story in the Hebrew language. Additionally, the way in which the Septuagint—an ancient Greek translation (third century B.C.) of the Hebrew text—rendered 1:9 is further evidence that those in the ancient world took pains to connect the Jonah at the beginning of our little book with the prophet Jonah alluded to in 2 Kings. Similarly, early rabbinic interpretation unanimously connects the prophet of the book of Jonah to the prophet of 2 Kings 14.

Although one should recognize that this connection between Jonah 1 and 2 Kings 14 is one of the most difficult issues in interpreting the book, the connection should not be quickly dismissed. As already stated above, the narrator has given us the story of Jonah to be read in proximity with the reign of Jeroboam II (786–746 B.C.). We do not know how long our protagonist lived, yet his life, or at least his influence, seems to have overlapped with Jeroboam II's reign. Therefore, it behooves us as readers to ask how God was interacting with the world during this period and, more specifically, how God was dealing with his covenant people during this historical period and why.

Jonah's mission occurred during the Israelite theocracy under the Mosaic period. Theocracy is the grid through which this period is to be understood. God had crafted this particular nation to be the apple of his eye. He had entered into a special covenantal relationship with them, setting the people and their land apart from all others to demonstrate that he would be their God and they would be his people.

This was the essence of covenant. Israel alone was Yahweh's treasured possession (*segullah*), a term pregnant in meaning especially now that we know its Akkadian cognates.[10] It seems that this term originally had to do with physical and private savings, but was extended to include a spiritual sense of being attached "to objects diligently and patiently acquired. Thus *segullah* comes to mean a dear personal possession, a 'treasure' only in the sense of that which is treasured or cherished."[11] This fits well with the biblical contexts (see also Deut. 7:6; 14:2; 26:18; Ps. 135:4; Mal. 3:17).

In Israel, at this particular time, there would be a theocracy that would find its reason for existence in the fact that God had chosen to dwell in the midst of this particular people among all the nations of the earth. God's dominion would be visible and external in a special manner. In other words, the reign of God could be seen in the geopolitical dimension in Israel and Judah. Although God has always ruled over his whole creation throughout all times by virtue of his providence and general care, a particular locale would especially be God's holy realm in this historical period. Here, among all the places in the earth, divinely sanctioned theocracy existed. As one Israeli biblical historian sums it up:

> The Pentateuch and historical books (Former Prophets), for example, consistently represent the world as divided into two realms, Israel and the nations, with Israel alone "the portion of YHWH." Deuteronomy goes so far as to assert that YHWH himself has "allotted" the worship of the host of heaven to the heathen (Deut. 4:19). . . . Thus while YHWH governs and manifests his activity everywhere—in Sodom, Shinar, Egypt, Nineveh and Tarshish—the area of his sanctity is restricted to the boundaries of Israel. The rest of the lands are the domain of the idols, the host of heaven, or the *shedim*—"no-gods" (Deut. 32:17). The early cult is entirely restricted to the sanctified territory of Israel (except for the desert cult, performed in a kind of portable sacred area). Outside it there is no sacrifice and no festival, but only impure ground where idols are worshiped.[12]

God's kingdom rule in the Israelite theocracy was not merely the invisible rule in people's hearts at this point in time; in this period of redemptive history, his reign was visible and earthly in the land of Israel. There, God's name would dwell.

According to Exodus 19:3–6, God revealed to Moses his divine blueprint for the theocracy:

> Then Moses went up to God, and the LORD called to him from the mountain and said, "This is what you are to say to the house of Jacob and what you are to tell the people of Israel: 'You yourselves have seen what I did to Egypt, and how I carried you on eagles'

wings and brought you to myself. Now if you obey me fully and keep my covenant, then out of all nations you will be my treasured possession [*segullah*]. Although the whole earth is mine, you will be for me a kingdom of priests and a holy nation.' These are the words you are to speak to the Israelites.''

This is the essence of God's relationship to this people: "I will be your God, and you will be my people." Israel is God's servant. Privilege also entails responsibility. This chosen people of God, the theocracy of Israel, was to set apart God's name before the surrounding nations. Theocracy entailed a mission, a mission that implied certain distinctiveness.

It is against this backdrop that the relationship between Israel and the Gentiles is brought to the foreground. Israel must distinguish herself in many ways from the surrounding nations. She must distinguish herself religiously from the surrounding nations. Although other nations may serve and worship many other gods, Israel is to serve only one (Deut. 6:4–19). Accordingly, there must be unequivocal commitment to the Lord's command: worship God alone at the place he chooses (Deut. 12). This command became crucial for how the kingdom of Israel and Judah and her kings would fare in the future.

During this period God will bless his chosen people if they do not go whoring after other gods. The nations will note that Israel is different and fear her (Deut. 28:8–10). Israel is to unswervingly obey the law. Other nations may practice all kinds of perverse ethical practices, but Israel must be marked off by purity of ethical behavior according to God's holy standard. Otherwise the land will vomit them out (Lev. 18:24–30).

Furthermore, within this theocratic relationship between God and his people, Israel had a temporary set of cultic regulations (i.e., ceremonial distinctiveness) and judicial practices (see the Westminster Confession of Faith 19.3–4). Israel was constituted a nation with a special purpose conditioned by the period in which she found herself; therefore, she had a distinctive, albeit temporal, set of ceremonial and judicial practices that were followed.

God had promised Abraham a land as well (Gen. 15:18–21). We begin to see partial fulfillment of that promise during this time. Israel's charter did not entail world domination; her charter did encompass, during that particular historical period, the subjection of the land of Canaan and the defeat of the Canaanite peoples who practiced idolatry. At that period in world history, then, a particular parcel of land in the world was divinely sanctioned as God's own possession for the dwelling of his name. However, when the theocracy passed away (we are using "theocracy" in this book to mean more than just the time of the monarchy; rather, in a general sense, the concept of theocracy may apply to the period before the monarchy, the monarchy itself, and even the postexilic period as well), so did the judicial and penal sanctions associated with it. When the theocracy passed away, so did the ceremonial regulations. Additionally, the divinely sanctioned geopolitical domination, that is, conquering land for Israel on behalf of God and subduing the Canaanites, also passed away. Shadows and types pass away once the substance has come. Fulfillment brings cessation. Christ brought fulfillment. Christ is the fulfillment.

As Clowney notes, the establishment of a distinct kingdom with an earthly king is a further development within the theocratic period. In the military battles of David, which culminated in the building of the temple by Solomon his son, the climax of the theocratic program becomes clear. David, a mighty warrior, has subdued the enemies of the land. He builds up the kingdom and places his capital in Jerusalem. It is left to Solomon, a man of peace, to erect the temple where God's name would preeminently dwell. Under

Solomon the temple is constructed as the dwelling place of God. God makes his abode in the midst of his people.

The temple demonstrates the grandeur and splendor of the kingdom. The surrounding nations will sit up and take notice of something markedly different in this little kingdom, as evidenced in Solomon's famous prayer dedicating the temple:

> As for the foreigner who does not belong to your people Israel but has come from a distant land because of your name—for men will hear of your great name and your mighty hand and your outstretched arm—when he comes and prays toward this temple, then hear from heaven, your dwelling place, and do whatever the foreigner asks of you, so that all the peoples of the earth may know your name and fear you, as do your own people Israel, and may know that this house I have built bears your Name. (1 Kings 8:41–43)

Solomon goes on to conclude his sublime prayer with a similar thought:

> And may these words of mine, which I have prayed before the LORD, be near to the LORD our God day and night, that he may uphold the cause of his servant and the cause of his people Israel according to each day's need, so that all the peoples of the earth may know that the LORD is God and that there is no other. But your hearts must be fully committed to the LORD our God, to live by his decrees and obey his commands, as at this time. (1 Kings 8:59–61)

If Solomon signifies the apex of the kingdom (although he himself was by no means the perfect king; see 1 Kings 11:7–13), beginning with Solomon and those kings following in his path a slippery slope spirals downward with only a few exceptions. From the perspective of the unknown author of the book of Kings, the kingdom is rent in two because of the syncretism and idolatry of the people. Following the reign of Solomon (1 Kings 2:12–11:43), the Northern tribes seceded and apostatized (1 Kings 12–14). King Jeroboam erected golden calves—one in Bethel and one in Dan—with the effect of drawing the people's affections away from Jerusalem and the temple (1 Kings 12:25–33). Jeroboam committed other atrocities that are portrayed negatively as violations of God's will. Nevertheless, God did not turn his back upon the people despite their unfaithfulness to the covenant.

Soon thereafter, Baal worship becomes a threat in the North at least temporarily. During the reign of Ahab and his wicked wife Jezebel, daughter of Ethbaal, king of the Sidonians, Baal worship is a dangerous attraction to Israel. Israel turns time and again from her God. If the people will not showcase God's glory by maintaining ritual, ceremonial, ethical, and geographical distinctiveness before the nations, then God like a faithful father will discipline her by means of other nations. If the Israelites play the part of an unfaithful spouse, then God, Israel's only true husband, will prosecute his covenantal lawsuit against the Israelites. And his servants the prophets do indeed prosecute the lawsuit (see, for example, Amos and Hosea).

It is important to our understanding of Jonah to recognize that during this time period, the blessings of two great Old Testament prophets had already come to the Gentiles. Elijah's prophetic work as described in 1 Kings 17 had blessed a Gentile widow in Zarephath, a place within the borders of Phoenicia, not Israel. Through this narrative the point is driven home: God's sovereignty reigns outside the borders of Israel. Already present in the Old Testament, mission finds its justification for going outside of the borders of Israel.

In Elisha's ministry also (Elijah's successor), the grace of God was extended beyond the borders of Israel: Naaman, a Syrian general (and Israel's enemy), received the blessings of God by being healed of his leprosy (2 Kings 5). The prophetic word was received with a welcome outside the borders of Israel, an allusion used so poignantly by our Lord that all his audience was filled with fury (Luke 4:27–29). There are, then, two sides to this coin. At the same time that blessings come to the Gentiles, judgment comes upon Israel.

The parallels between these prophets and Jonah should be noted. Toward the end of Elijah's ministry (1 Kings 19), he was directed to do three things: anoint Hazael as king over Aram, anoint Jehu as king over Israel, and anoint Elisha as prophet to succeed him. The latter Elijah did (in a certain sense), but the former two things he did not do. Did this thwart God's plan? No.

It was Elisha, Elijah's successor, who brought the news to Hazael that he would become king in Aram and, furthermore, that as the new king, Hazael would wreak havoc on Israel:

Elisha went to Damascus, and Ben-Hadad king of Aram was ill. When the king was told, "The man of God has come all the way up here," he said to Hazael, "Take a gift with you and go to meet the man of God. Consult the LORD through him; ask him, 'Will I recover from this illness?' "

Hazael went to meet Elisha, taking with him as a gift forty camel-loads of all the finest wares of Damascus. He went in and stood before him, and said, "Your son Ben-Hadad king of Aram has sent me to ask, 'Will I recover from this illness?' "

Elisha answered, "Go and say to him, 'You will certainly recover'; but the LORD has revealed to me that he will in fact die." He stared at him with a fixed gaze until Hazael felt ashamed. Then the man of God [i.e., Elisha!] began to weep.

"Why is my lord weeping?" asked Hazael.

"Because I know the harm you will do to the Israelites," he answered. "You will set fire to their fortified places, kill their young men with the sword, dash their little children to the ground, and rip open their pregnant women."

Hazael said, "How could your servant, a mere dog, accomplish such a feat?"

"The LORD has shown me that you will become king of Aram," answered Elisha. (2 Kings 8:7–13)

This word of the Lord was fulfilled. In 2 Kings 13:22 we read, "Hazael king of Aram oppressed Israel throughout the reign of Jehoahaz." No wonder that Elisha's message brought such grief to the prophet. It was a bitter duty for him to discharge. Elisha's own people were to suffer judgment at the hands of the Gentiles. Elisha himself was the harbinger of bad news for his own people.

Now just as Elisha loathed going to Hazael, a future Gentile king who would bring judgment upon Israel, it is possible that Jonah also loathed going to Nineveh for similar reasons. For, according to the prophets, Assyria would be the instrument in God's hand against the Israelites. Blessings come to the Gentiles (Nineveh in Jonah's case), but God brings judgment upon Israel through the Gentiles. Furthermore, Jonah knows God's character (Jonah 4:2). So the charge to go to Nineveh was possibly repugnant to Jonah.[13]

Perhaps the Nobel Prize–winning author, Elie Wiesel, had it right when he gave our poor antihero the benefit of the doubt and wrote that Jonah "does not wish Nineveh to die, yet he does not wish Nineveh to live at the expense of Israel."[14] This was by no means the only possible reason why Jonah didn't want to go to Nineveh. Many commentators have noted other reasons as well.

Although there are judgment and chastisement, the book of Jonah is heavy with mercy. Jonah should have observed that there was mercy for him and that there would be mercy for the people of Israel as well. God showed great mercy while he pursued Jonah sleeping on the ship. Indeed, God rescued him. The reader can recognize in hindsight that another place we can see this mercy is in the exile and eventual restoration of Israel to its land. Moreover, the prophets declared that there would be mercy for those outside of Israel. We begin to see mercy in even fuller measure when we turn to the New Testament.

As in the rest of Scripture, judgment and mercy are both observed in the book of Jonah. Much more will be said about this in the pages that follow. Chastisement comes to Israel by foreign nations because she repeatedly broke covenant with her Lord. Mercy, however, is extended to the Gentiles as a corollary response. Indeed, mercy is primary, but never at the expense of justice, for God must be true.

Indeed, Nineveh is blessed. The mercies of God are extended to the Gentiles as well as the Hebrews. The promise previously announced to Abraham (Gen. 12:1–3), namely, that all the nations will be blessed, is taking further shape in preparation for the coming of the greatest prophet: Jesus Christ. The Old Testament is heavy with eschatology. With respect to the future, Nineveh will become the symbol of great rebuke against Israel (Matt. 12:41). Nineveh will also become a great symbol of mercy to the Gentiles.

## THE MESSAGE OF THE BOOK OF JONAH

Jonah's message has been hammered out upon the anvil of many different interpretations through the ages.

Sometimes anti-Semitism got the better of people. Sometimes their imaginations did. The traditions of the rabbis actually connected Jonah with the unidentified son of the widow of Zarephath (1 Kings 17). As alluded to earlier, the unbridled imaginations of the early church fathers concocted far-fetched meanings. Augustine saw Jonah as pointing forward to Christ, but also as a sign of the still immature Jewish nation not yet emerged into the full bloom of the Christian church.

Luther in preparation for his lectures on the book of Jonah found it difficult to escape a negative presentation of old Israel. Calvin saw the book essentially as an object lesson from the schoolhouse of discipline: Jonah provides an example of a necessary attitude adjustment for the wayward, errant, or backsliding saint. The Enlightenment brought in the theme of universalism, that is, God's love and mercy extending beyond the borders of national Israel. In the nineteenth century, many interpreters tried to turn the little book into a textbook of biology by myopically focusing on the nature, size, and plausibility of the great fish that swallowed the prophet. Finally, some postmodern interpreters foreground the threat of a "Christian colonization" of the Old Testament and warn against the New Testament exercising hegemony over the Old Testament.

What message or messages one derives from the little prophecy of Jonah is largely relative to the interpretive principles one applies to the text. The message one receives from the book of Jonah is also directly related to the questions one asks.

The book of Jonah, even on a superficial reading, is obviously taking pains to demonstrate God's mercy to those outside of Israel, as discussed above. But why? This message will find its culminating fulfillment in the person and work of Jesus Christ. In other words, whereas the advent of the Lord of history as recorded in the four Gospels discloses the inauguration of the kingdom of God in new fullness, a kingdom which will include both Jews and Gentiles to the ends of the earth, the book of Jonah presages that earth-shaking event many centuries in advance of its actual occurrence.

But mercy is communicated not only to those outside of Israel. Indeed, many scholars have recognized the theme of mercy in the immediate context of 2 Kings 14:25. The reader should note the goodness of God that was extended toward Israel:

> He [i.e., Jeroboam II] was the one who restored the boundaries of Israel from Lebo Hamath to the Sea of the Arabah, in accordance with the word of the LORD, the God of Israel, spoken through his servant Jonah son of Amittai, the prophet from Gath Hepher.
>
> The LORD had seen how bitterly everyone in Israel, whether slave or free, was suffering; there was no one to help them. And since the LORD had not said he would blot out the name of Israel from under heaven, he saved them by the hand of Jeroboam son of Jehoash. (2 Kings 14:25–27)

But notice the immediate context of these verses! The author says, "He [i.e., Jeroboam II] did evil in the eyes of the LORD and did not turn away from any of the sins of Jeroboam son of Nebat, which he had caused Israel to commit" (2 Kings 14:24). In sum, God has been merciful to Israel as well as to Nineveh.

There are other messages in the book of Jonah. Usually the commentaries give a range of views pigeonholing various authors accordingly. Indeed, this little book of Jonah is not intended to communicate merely a message, but messages. The book of Jonah is a highly complex and artistic short story as recent studies have demonstrated.

Therefore, in order to take in the kaleidoscope of lessons found in the book, the reader must approach the text with a teachable attitude. A good student will be a reader who is persuadable and listens quietly and calmly, proceeding slowly, meditatively. This is not easy for us moderns. It is like climbing a mountain. It takes painstaking effort and self-discipline, but the rewards at the end are worth the effort. If one expects to learn from Jonah, then one must properly prepare to read it, and preparation entails openness and humility.

## FOR FURTHER REFLECTION

1. When was Jonah written?
2. What can be said about the authorship of Jonah?
3. What is a covenant, and why is it important for interpreting the book of Jonah even though explicit references to the word are absent?
4. Summarize the history of the ministry of the following prophets: Elijah, Elisha, and Jonah. How are their ministries similar and how different? Why is this important for understanding the book of Jonah?

# 2

## THE RUNAWAY PROPHET

## ( 1 : 1 – 3 )

Consider, once more, the universal cannibalism of the sea; all whose creatures prey upon each other, carrying on eternal war since the world began. Consider all this; and then turn to this green, gentle, and most docile earth; consider them both, the sea and the land; and do you not find a strange analogy to something in yourself? For as this appalling ocean surrounds the verdant land, so in the soul of man there lies one insular Tahiti, full of peace and joy, but encompassed by all the horrors of the half known life. God keep thee! Push not off from that isle, thou canst never return! (Herman Melville, *Moby Dick*)

The word of the LORD came to Jonah son of Amittai: "Go to the great city of Nineveh and preach against it, because its wickedness has come up before me."

But Jonah ran away from the LORD and headed for Tarshish. He went down to Joppa, where he found a ship bound for that port. After paying the fare, he went

aboard and sailed for Tarshish to flee from the Lord.
(Jonah 1:1–3)


## JONAH THE PROPHET AND
## THE REPRESENTATIVE OF ISRAEL

The opening lines are absolutely crucial in any story, and especially in a world where stories carry neither a title page nor a table of contents. Although in the first verse we are introduced to the only character in this short story who receives a name, Jonah the son of Amittai, we are not given very much information about him. As Elie Wiesel once wrote:

> His file in Scripture is astonishingly meager. His name, and the name of his father and nothing else. Where does he dwell? Mystery. Who are his friends, his teachers, his enemies? Impossible to ascertain. What was he doing until the incident that made him famous? What became of him afterwards? Nobody tells us. Without Nineveh and its sinners, Jonah might not have figured in sacred Jewish History— and neither would the whale.[1]

The name *Yonah ben 'Amittay* means "Dove, son of truth." Usually the ancient Semites were very thoughtful and deliberate about the names they chose for their children; often a person's name was freighted with tremendous significance. Although some authors see varying degrees of importance in Jonah's name, my own opinion is that this should not be overinterpreted. It would be easy for a modern reader to make hay of such an epithet after reading the story of this prophet, but scarce data and thousands of years separating us from the ancient author should breed a note of caution about doing so. The main character's name was Jonah. Just as our actions contribute to our name, so this protagonist's actions, whose name happens to be Jonah son of Amittai, describe his character more than do conjectures about the meaning or etymology of the words that make up his name.

Even so, why is Jonah's biography so thin? This is an important interpretive question for the rest of the book. In the previous chapter, I discussed the subject of who the original audience may have been. Although we cannot say for sure who the immediate audience was, we can say that the author was speaking to Israel in the Old Testament and to God's church in each succeeding generation. We need to say something more about this point that the book addresses Israel particularly.

If it is true that Jonah is addressed, at least initially, to the people of God in the Old Testament (i.e., Israel), then is it possible that Jonah plays a representative role in some sense? Other prophets in the Old Testament did so (e.g., Hosea and Ezekiel), and I do think together with some other interpreters of this book that indeed Jonah does play a representative role.[2]

Many years ago Calvin Seminary professor John Stek suggested that there are three possibilities for Jonah's representational role: he may be representing people in general (several writers take this position), he may be representing anyone to whom a prophetic role has been given, or he may be representing Israel as a whole nation.[3] Stek argues successfully, in my opinion, for the last option.

Jonah was not representing every person, although at times the reader can definitely identify with Jonah. This is the case especially with his foolishness or stubbornness. Moreover, we will see when we turn to the second chapter of Jonah in particular, that the poetry draws us in to sympathize and actually identify with the prophet.

Nor was Jonah representing every prophet in Israel. Rather, Jonah represented all Israel. This position is bolstered in many ways according to Stek: we are told very little about the man Jonah, very little is said about the prophetic office, and the whole episode is played out on the vast stage of the world, first with the sailors and then with Nineveh itself, which seems to represent the Gentiles. Stek offers other evidences as well, and the reader is encouraged to read his article to understand his position.

Edmund Clowney makes a similar point when he says, "Jonah as the individual servant of the Lord represents the whole nation called to be God's servant."[4] God intended to say something to the Israelites about their relationship with the Gentiles, and through them God also intended to say something about Israel's relationship to God even before the coming of Christ. Here was direct application for the Israelites. The message of Jonah is not merely a rebuke to Jonah the prophet, but is also a rebuke to the whole nation of Israel whom Jonah represents. This will become especially evident as we turn to the fourth chapter of Jonah. This interpretation of Jonah, however, needs to be handled carefully for it can lead one down the path of allegorical interpretation.

## NINEVEH THE GREAT CITY

If Jonah represents the entire nation of Israel in a certain sense, then it is also true that Nineveh represents the entire world of the Gentiles in a certain sense. As Professor Stek notes, this is especially the case in chapter 4 where the pity that God expresses toward the Ninevites and their animals can be extended appropriately to the wider world.

God commands Jonah to go to the great ancient city of Nineveh. This city was one of the greatest in the ancient world. Located about six hundred miles northeast of Israel, it endured for over a thousand years. Nineveh was huge by ancient standards. This is indicated by the fine details and accents in the Hebrew language as well as by what we know from the archeology of the ancient city.

The city was located in what is now northern Iraq, near present-day Al-Mawsil (Mosul). In the nineteenth century, British archeologists conducted excavations which yielded many inscriptions and magnificent reliefs now securely housed at the famous British Museum. The Iraqi government continued excavations in the region throughout the 1960s and 1970s. Therefore, we now know a fair amount about the site. Indeed, Nineveh has become one of the most important sites for informing us in the modern world about ancient Assyrian practices.

During Sennacherib's reign (704–681 B.C.), Nineveh became the chief royal city of the Assyrian Empire (2 Kings 19:36), with magnificent buildings and walls. The city was finally destroyed in August of 612 B.C. by the Medes. Soon afterward, the Babylonians occupied the city. In the years that followed, Nineveh became a symbol representing the forces of evil arrayed against the people of God much as Babylon became such a symbol later in the book of Revelation.[5] The city, and the mere mention of its name, retained its negative impact upon the memory of the Hebrews long after the city's destruction. Even in the early church, Nineveh came to be regarded as a symbol of the devil himself.[6] Given this background, the reader can imagine the thoughts that would have been uppermost in Jonah's mind when he received this commission from God: "Go to the great city of Nineveh and preach against it."

## GOD'S COMMAND AND JONAH'S RESPONSE

Jonah was commanded to do one thing: Go and preach against Nineveh. God's expression of his sovereign will is a commission to Jonah: Get up and go! We expect this prophet of God to comply from what we know of previous prophets' responses to God's commissions. In 1 Kings we read, "Then the word of the LORD came to Elijah: 'Leave here, turn eastward and hide in the Kerith Ravine'" (1 Kings 17:2). In verse 5, we read that Elijah did just as he had been expected to do: "So he did what the LORD had told him. He went to the Kerith Ravine" (1 Kings 17:5). What a stark contrast Jonah portrays.

The response of a compliant person to the command of God (or to another speaker of higher status) is often echoed in similar-sounding narrative forms built from the same verbal roots in the Hebrew narrative. Therefore, in verse 3 we expect to read that Jonah *got up and went.* Instead we read that he *got up in order to flee.* In fact, Jonah is so determined to run away from God that the writer shows in detail how determined Jonah was in his efforts.

First, he goes to Joppa, modern-day Jaffa, which is a port city not far from modern Tel Aviv. During ancient times Joppa remained outside Hebrew control except for a very brief time. Consequently, as interpreters have recognized for centuries, Jonah is apparently seeking to avoid God's oversight by fleeing to this city.

Second, he boards a Tarshish-bound ship. While the location of Tarshish is much disputed, one thing is agreed upon by all: Tarshish is in exactly the opposite direction of Nineveh. While God commanded Jonah to go eastward, Jonah took it upon himself to tuck tail and run westward. This is the beginning of Jonah's long downfall.

Third, travel by sea in the ancient world took a very long time since a ship could travel only at a painstakingly slow pace (by today's standards), and the season for safe traveling was limited to a few months out of the year. The conclusion is that Jonah was trying to escape from God's sovereign control. Therefore, our book begins with tension: the formal expression of God's sovereign will ("get up and go") versus the prophet's determined opposition to that declaration ("he got up and fled"). If there is any doubt left, notice that our narrator has focused our attention on the fact that Jonah was fleeing literally "from the presence of the LORD" (mentioned twice in verse 3). It is not merely disobedience, however, that is Jonah's problem. Disobedience is merely the presenting problem if you will. There are more fundamental issues lurking below the surface of his behavior.

Before the reader yields to the temptation to frown upon our antihero, we must recognize that the same impulse is found in all of our hearts: flight from obedience to God and flight from service of our Lord. Years ago, Abraham Kuyper, journalist, Reformed theologian, and onetime prime minister of the Netherlands, summarized the human condition well: "Our heart is continually inclined to rebel against the Lord our God. So ready to rebel, that O, so gladly, were it but for a single day, we would take from His hands the reins of His supreme rule, imagining that we would manage things far better and direct them far more effectively than God."[7]

The orientation and setting are now complete; we have been introduced to the scene and the main character. The author of Jonah has expressed so much with so few words. Moreover, we have been introduced to one of the most crucial questions of the story: Why did Jonah flee?

## FOR FURTHER REFLECTION

1. What do we know about Jonah? How does Jonah represent more than himself?
2. What role does Assyria play in the Bible?
3. What might an ancient Israelite have thought when the city of Nineveh was mentioned?
4. How do the opening three verses of Jonah serve as an introduction to the whole book?

# 3

## PANDEMONIUM
## ABOARD THE SHIP (1:4–6)

When every moment we thought the ship would sink!
Death and Judgement then? What? With all three masts
making such an everlasting thundering against the side;
and every sea breaking over us, fore and aft. Think of
Death and the Judgement then? No! (Herman Melville,
*Moby Dick*)

Then the LORD sent a great wind on the sea, and such a
violent storm arose that the ship threatened to break
up. All the sailors were afraid and each cried out to his
own god. And they threw the cargo into the sea to
lighten the ship.
  But Jonah had gone below deck, where he lay down
and fell into a deep sleep. The captain went to him and
said, "How can you sleep? Get up and call on your god!
Maybe he will take notice of us, and we will not perish."
(Jonah 1:4–6)

When we come to verse 4, a new scene opens before our eyes. The narrator takes pains to demonstrate that Jonah's designs will not be as smoothly executed as perhaps he had thought. The word order in Hebrew is not what is normally expected. Here the language focuses our attention upon the counteraction taken by the subject, namely, the Lord: "But the LORD sent." The Lord has control of the high ground as well as the sea in this challenge with the prophet.

The Israelites had virtually no or very little experience upon the open sea. They were mostly landlocked land-lubbers, although a few cryptic comments in Scripture would suggest otherwise (1 Kings 22:48–49; 2 Chron. 9:21; 20:35–37; and Ps. 107:23–32, for example) and Solomon had developed a navy. We do know something about ancient maritime practices in the countries surrounding Israel, but trying to read these customs into the book of Jonah is an elusive endeavor.

Yet, on the basis of the text before us and our knowledge of seafaring in the ancient Near East, we can assert this much: storms at sea must have held a great degree of captivation and awe for the Israelites. Indeed, in the biblical book of Ezekiel there is a lament for the city of Tyre (a Phoenician trading post) that illustrates Israel's fascination with the sea:

> The ships of Tarshish serve
>   as carriers for your wares.
> You are filled with heavy cargo
>   in the heart of the sea.
> Your oarsmen take you
>   out to the high seas.
> But the east wind will break you to pieces
>   in the heart of the sea.
> Your wealth, merchandise and wares,
>   your mariners, seamen and shipwrights,

> your merchants and all your soldiers,
> > and everyone else on board
> will sink into the heart of the sea
> > on the day of your shipwreck.
> The shorelands will quake
> > when your seamen cry out. . . .
> Now you are shattered by the sea
> > in the depths of the waters;
> your wares and all your company
> > have gone down with you. (Ezek. 27:25–28, 34)

Contrary to some writers' assertions, it is not immediately evident that the Ezekiel tradition is a source for the Jonah narrative, though there are many parallels.

The storm must have been ferocious because men experienced on the sea do not grow uneasy quickly at the first sight of foul weather. For many years, I witnessed this as a commercial fisherman on the waters of Alaska. During those years, I was often impressed by the calm that would come over experienced fishermen even while the wind howled and the sea grew tumultuous and waves slapped over the gunwales. Here these sailors are frantic, and that tells us that this was no ordinary storm. Indeed, a theme of fear is carefully woven throughout this first chapter (see verses 5, 10, and 16).

The narrator takes pains to describe this storm as God-sent. The storm raged. This storm was so savage that the ship herself threatened to break apart. Personification is applied to the ship. This may not be immediately apparent in translation, but the excellent biblical scholar, Jack Sasson, comes closer to the original language when he translates, "The ship *expected itself* to crack up."[1] Or, as another author says (with tongue in cheek?), the ship is about to become a "nervous wreck."[2] This is a commonplace writing technique of many of the world's literatures, including the Bible, and therefore it should not seem strange to the reader. In fact, in the book of Isaiah some Tarshish ships are commanded to wail (see Isa. 23:1).

In order to support artistically the description of the ship being tortured by the storm, the narrator has made the Hebrew at the end of verse 4 sound like waves crashing against the vessel (*hishebah lehishaber*). The Hebrews had a knack for making puns with their language (as did other peoples speaking and writing in various Semitic languages). Often a theological or literary nuance is driven home by such a pun.

So frightened are these sailors by this terrible storm that one experienced man after another cries out to his own god, and they even begin to jettison their cargo. These sailors are not innocent bystanders (pace some commentators) caught up in the counteraction of a deity in hot pursuit of his aberrant prophet. Their own idolatries qualify them as the object of God's wrath (Rom. 3:10–18). Just after reading that the Lord "sent" (literally, "threw") a huge wind upon the sea, we read that the sailors "threw" (the same Hebrew verb) some of their cargo overboard. Soon, they will be throwing (the same Hebrew verb) a passenger over the sides as well in order to appease the sea.

Not all of those on board, however, are frantic. The wind howls, the waves crash, the spray hisses, the ship is foundering, the sailors reel; meanwhile, Jonah goes down and falls fast asleep below. The text shifts its focus from the response of the sailors to the storm to the response of Jonah.

The NIV translation of verse 5 suggests that Jonah had already gone down below before the storm broke out. The Hebrew text is not this specific, and I'm inclined to think for several reasons that Jonah went down at the same time the storm broke and the seamen were striving to save the ship. The sailors respond to the storm with action while Jonah responds with inaction.

The progressive descent of Jonah is echoed with puns throughout this passage. In verse 3 Jonah *went down* (*vayyered*) to Joppa and *then went down* (*vayyered*) into the ship. Now in verse 5 Jonah has *gone down* (*yarad*) again in order to *find sweet sleep* (*vayyeradam*). What a contrast between the sleeping prophet hunkered down below and the scene of pandemonium that exists above. The narrator's choice of words here indicates more than light sleep; on the contrary, the verbs and nouns associated with this Hebrew word have to do with a deep or hypnotic sleep (e.g., Gen. 2:21; Job 4:13; Judg. 4:21). The Septuagint, an ancient Greek translation of the Hebrew text, actually inserts an editorial comment at this point and says that Jonah, our sleeping antihero, began to snore! It is probably foolhardy to venture too far into the exact nature of this sleep. This has often resulted only in speculations about Jonah's psychological state.

Now the captain of the ship (or perhaps a "helmsman") descends so that he might implore the sleepyhead to call upon his god in order that they and the boat should not perish. As the polytheistic Athenians feared leaving any god unappeased and erected an altar to "an unknown god" (Acts 17:23), exactly so the captain of the ship now appeals to the groggy prophet to placate his god as well. The captain questions Jonah, "How can you sleep?" He uses a Hebrew idiom (*mah-lleka*), that influences New Testament speech as well (John 2:4) and that signifies some kind of reproof, "What is the matter with you?" An audience that knows Hebrew may very well hear an echo in verse 6 of the puns just made in the previous verses since the captain says, "What is the matter with you, *sleeper*?" (*nirdam*).

In spite of the danger into which the wayward prophet has thrown the captain and his crew, Jonah does not even respond to the captain at this point. Additionally, the captain's comments—"*maybe* he [God] will take note of us"—possibly introduce us to another important theme developed throughout the story: God's free actions apart from human behavior.

In the past two chapters, we have been carefully observing the characterization of this prophet in flight. Jonah has disobeyed the clear command of God. Furthermore, he has dangerously involved others in his escapism. How different this prophet's behavior is from the behavior of a Prophet who would later come from Israel.

Jonah's behavior not only presents a stark contrast to the sailors, but his actions also differ greatly from those of Jesus, the prophet from Nazareth (Matt. 21:11; Luke 7:16; John 4:19). Jacques Ellul thoughtfully comments on the differences between Jonah and Christ: "There are, of course, great differences between Jonah and Jesus Christ. Jonah is guilty. Jonah did not want to do God's will. Jonah is not Jesus Christ, just as Joshua and David are not Jesus Christ. But he is one of the long line of types of Jesus, each representing an aspect of what the Son of God will be in totality."[3] Unlike the recalcitrant prophet in flight from service to God, Jesus was a prophet who delighted to discharge all his duty before his heavenly Father. Indeed, Jesus never balked in his commitment to do the Father's will (John 17:4; Phil. 2:6–8).

Notice as well the behavior of Jonah in the storm in contrast to our Lord in the midst of a storm on the Sea of Galilee (Matt. 8:23–27; Mark 4:35–41; Luke 8:22–25). While both sleep in the midst of the danger, the rest of those in the boat are panic-stricken. The disciples in the boat with Jesus are afraid because they have lost faith. The sailors aboard the boat with Jonah are afraid because they think they are lost, but they are thus far in the story unaware of who it is who has brought such chaos crashing down on them.

Jonah, a mere man, seeks to escape the will of God and the storm by going below and falling into a deep sleep. Jesus, more than a mere man, sleeps through the storm because he has fully embraced the will of his heavenly Father. On the one hand, Jonah runs from the duties of his prophetic office. On the other hand, Jesus is in full control of discharging the duties of his office and rebukes not only the disciples for their loss of faith but also the waves, resulting in a calming influence over the raging sea. This comparison reveals the contrast: a vast gulf between the Creator-Redeemer and the creature.

## FOR FURTHER REFLECTION

1. How familiar were the Israelites with the sea?
2. What details indicate the severity of this storm?
3. How would you compare the behavior of Jonah with the behavior of the sailors?
4. How would you compare the behavior of Jonah as a prophet with the behavior of Christ the prophet?
5. Can you think of any ways in which these first six verses of Jonah are preparing you for other aspects of the story that are coming?

# 4

## PROPHET OVERBOARD

### ( 1 : 7 – 1 6 )

But, alas! the practices of whalemen soon convinced him that even Christians could be both miserable and wicked; infinitely more so, than all his father's heathens. (Herman Melville, *Moby Dick*)

Then the sailors said to each other, "Come, let us cast lots to find out who is responsible for this calamity." They cast lots and the lot fell on Jonah.

So they asked him, "Tell us, who is responsible for making all this trouble for us? What do you do? Where do you come from? What is your country? From what people are you?"

He answered, "I am a Hebrew and I worship the LORD, the God of heaven, who made the sea and the land."

This terrified them and they asked, "What have you done?" (They knew he was running away from the LORD, because he had already told them so.)

The sea was getting rougher and rougher. So they asked him, "What should we do to you to make the sea calm down for us?"

"Pick me up and throw me into the sea," he replied, "and it will become calm. I know that it is my fault that this great storm has come upon you."

Instead, the men did their best to row back to land. But they could not, for the sea grew even wilder than before. Then they cried to the LORD, "O LORD, please do not let us die for taking this man's life. Do not hold us accountable for killing an innocent man, for you, O LORD, have done as you pleased." Then they took Jonah and threw him overboard, and the raging sea grew calm. At this the men greatly feared the LORD, and they offered a sacrifice to the LORD and made vows to him. (Jonah 1:7–16)

## THE STRUCTURE OF CHAPTER 1

In the last couple of chapters I have been orienting the reader to many issues raised by the book of Jonah: how the historical and theological background helps one read Jonah, the importance of responsible Christocentric reading of the Scriptures and appropriate application of the passage to the original and succeeding audiences, and different literary devices that the author uses in order to make the book fresh and engaging. In this chapter, I will introduce you to some further literary techniques often used by biblical authors. I will also address a fairly large piece of narrative from chapter 1 of Jonah and help the reader interpret this section in its immediate and canonical context.

Determining the structure of a biblical narrative is often very important for its meaning. Meaning is often communicated through the presentation of the patterns of words, phrases, and themes in a passage. Form and content should not be divorced from one another in the pursuit of meaning. In regard to form, chiasm is a literary figure that was often used by ancient writers. In a chiastic pattern, the elements in the second half of the structure invert the elements of the first half. The pattern may be long or short, very complex or very simple.[1] Just as scholars have noted chiasms in other Old Testament books, so too some have suggested chiasms in the book of Jonah.

Ever since Norbert Lohfink first suggested a concentric or chiastic pattern in the first chapter of Jonah, many others have suggested variations thereof. We will see chiasm employed in the second chapter of Jonah; however, many efforts at determining meaning and drawing conclusions regarding chapter 1 on the basis of a chiastic structure are often too strained.

## DETERMINING GOD'S WILL

Gaining insight into the divine will was different in the ancient world from the approaches employed today. Sometimes people found guidance for future decisions in the patterns in which birds flew. At other times, the ancients looked to the entrails of certain animals. We actually have many extant Babylonian liver omens in the Akkadian language. Graduate students studying ancient Semitic languages, including the ancient language of the Babylonians, sometimes have to endure the better part of an academic year interpreting Akkadian liver omens from Mesopotamia!

For ancient civilizations, determining the future or the reasons for certain occurrences might also involve examining various natural phenomena, including the patterns and cycles of nature. Another common mechanism for inquiring of heaven into mysterious phenomena was the practice of casting lots.

This practice of casting lots is referred to in several parts of the Bible (Lev. 16:8–10; Judg. 20:9; 1 Sam. 10:19–21;

Neh. 11:1; Prov. 18:18; Acts 1:26). It is difficult to determine what the exact procedure was. Nevertheless, the sense is clear despite the various methods employed: to be singled out by lot was to be divinely selected, or so it was believed. This is the method to which the sailors resort in the story of Jonah. Having received the answer that Jonah is their man, they proceed to press Jonah with questions.

In the Hebrew, it is evident the sailors know full well that it is Jonah who is responsible for bringing the present crisis upon them. Immediately they proceed to pepper him with questions: "What do you do [i.e., what's your mission]?" "Where do you come from?" "What is your country?" and "From what people are you?" There is a mysterious order to the questions here. In keeping with the idiom of the day, Jonah takes up their last question first. The credal statement in 1:9 and the credal statement given in 4:2 are literary cruxes. That is, they are extremely important to the story and must not be passed over lightly.

Jonah defines himself as an 'ibri, that is, a *Hebrew*. Although there were other terms of ethnic identification available, the narrator chooses the one most fitting for the context, that is, Jonah answering a foreigner. Jonah continues by employing the covenantal name of God. He goes on to say, "I worship the Lord, the God of heaven, who made the sea and the land" (v. 9). The order of the words in Hebrew actually focuses attention upon "the Lord." More literally (and woodenly) in Hebrew he declares, "The Lord, the God of the heavens, I fear, who made the sea and the dry ground." A few additional comments about this credal statement are in order.

First, the credal statement found on Jonah's tongue contains a literary device called a *merism*, that is, a statement of opposites in order to communicate totality. The crucial point about a merism is that both words of a merism must be studied together, as opposed to individually, in order to grasp the intended concept. Most languages employ this literary device in one way or another at various times. For example, in English when a person says that she has been sick "day and night," what she means to say is that she has been sick all the time. Similarly, when Jonah says, "I worship the LORD, the God of heaven, *who made the sea and the land*," he is saying, "the Creator of everything that exists."

Second, tension continues to build as Jonah subtly reverses the word order of the typical occurrence of this credal statement in the Bible: "sea" is out of its usual order. This underscores the extreme fear building among these sailors. The original audience would also pick up on the extreme fear of the sailors from the Hebrew construction used. Simply stated, when a Hebrew writer wishes to strengthen the verbal force of an expression, one method at his disposal is to use as the object of the verb a noun that is built from the same consonants as the verb. So when the NIV translates, "This terrified them," the actual expression is "The men *feared* a *great fear*."

The revelation by Jonah in verse 9 begins a whole chain of events that may not be immediately apparent to the reader, given the very pregnant and terse manner in which the narrative begins to unravel. Jonah's credal confession was probably followed by a fuller explanation of the events that had transpired in the recent past of his personal life (although unstated in our text). Following that, the sailors begin to understand that "he was running away from the LORD," so they exclaim, "What have you done?" This phrase is found in other contexts which have the tone of rebuke (see Gen. 20:9).

The sailors pummel Jonah with another question in verse 11, "What should we do to you to make the sea calm down for us?" A major interpretive question regarding verses 11 and 12 is whether the statement "the sea was getting rougher and rougher" actually stands within the quotation of the sailors or outside of their quotation as a comment in the narrative. It probably should stand inside the quotes (unlike the NIV quoted above) since Jonah seems to pick up the very language of the sailors in verse 12. It also suggests the anxious tone in which the sailors spoke.

Both the choice of vocabulary ("Pick me up") and the word order itself indicate that Jonah is not abdicating his role here; instead, he tells the sailors that if they do as he says, then the storm will abate and the sea will grow quiet. Given the text of verse 12, there is no doubt whatsoever that Jonah understands that he himself is responsible for the storm. Moreover, the legal language and overtones he uses assure the sailors that they will bear no responsibility for what they are instructed to do. However, do the sailors take his word at face value? No.

They don't seem to believe or trust him (or are they acting magnanimously toward him?). Instead they start rowing toward the shore in the middle of a ferocious storm! This was just as dangerous in the ancient world as it is in modern times, and maritime practices in the ancient world were probably the same then as they are now. A ship's well-being is more threatened by a storm or hurricane when it is harbored than when it is at sea, but these sailors go against all reason and turn for shore. They have just heard the prophet inform them that God controls the sea and the land (*hayyabbashah*), but now they try to dig in their oars and make for that same dry land (*hayyabbashah* again), which is most likely being buffeted by the crashing waves at this time.

Unable to row to shore, the sailors finally acquiesce since the sea is only growing more tumultuous. It is interesting to note that the grammar of the book of Jonah simultaneously seems to emphasize the futility of human efforts and the successful acts of God. More specifically, Jonathan Magonet has demonstrated that when an infinitive is used in the book of Jonah (a verbal form that, unlike finite verbs, is not constrained by person and number) to describe an action undertaken by humans (e.g., 1:3; 1:5; 1:13; 4:2), then those actions fail.[2] In contrast to this, when an infinitive is used of an action undertaken by God (e.g., 1:17; 4:6 twice), whatever is endeavored by the Almighty succeeds. (There is one exception to this pattern in 3:10b, with which Magonet dispatches.)

This takes us to the pinnacle of chapter 1, that is, verse 14. For the first time, the sailors now call on the name of the Hebrew God (*YHWH*). What a stark contrast this provides with what has gone before. Instead of each man calling on his own god (as in verse 5), now the narrator employs a Hebrew idiom (*qara 'el-YHWH*, "cry out to the Lord") which has been applied only to Jonah up to this point. Jonah will use this idiom again in his prayer from the depths in 2:2.

The sailors seem to be indicating that Jonah's statements do not yet convince them that they are free of all legal entailments (cf. Matt. 27:25). They are in a legal and ethical double bind: If they take the man's word at face value and perform it, then they may be guilty of murder; however, if they don't obey his word, not only are they contravening what the prophet has commanded them to do—the prophet who they know is responsible for their plight—they themselves might very well drown in the storm. They, as all of us often are, are caught in the dilemma of having to make a very important ethical choice with an amount of information that falls far short of absolute certitude.[3]

Now the sailors pray to the Hebrew God. They plead that they not perish, and they ask that they not be held guilty of innocent blood. The end of the sailors' prayer is most instructive especially in light of how the phrase is used in other biblical passages. The sailors declare, "For you, O Lord, have done as you pleased." As Thomas Bolin has pointed out, there are three other times when the Hebrew Bible says that God does whatever he pleases: Isaiah 46:10; Psalm 115:3; and Psalm 135:6.[4] The germane consideration here is the overlap of ideas with the book of Jonah. In each case, there are two significant points of overlap: the futility of worshiping idols and God's rule over all of creation. Consider first the passage from Isaiah:

> To whom will you compare me or count me equal?
>> To whom will you liken me that we may be
>>> compared?
> Some pour out gold from their bags
>> and weigh out silver on the scales;
> they hire a goldsmith to make it into a god,
>> and they bow down and worship it. . . .
> Though one cries out to it, it does not answer;
>> it cannot save him from his troubles.
> Remember this, fix it in mind,
>> take it to heart, you rebels.
> Remember the former things, those of long ago;
>> I am God, and there is no other;
>> I am God, and there is none like me.
> I make known the end from the beginning,
>> from ancient times, what is still to come.
> I say: My purpose will stand,
>> and I will *do all that I please*. (Isa. 46:5–10)

The two passages from the Psalms are also instructive:

> Our God is in heaven;
>> *he does whatever pleases him.*
> But their idols are silver and gold,
>> made by the hands of men. (Ps. 115:3–4)

> I know that the LORD is great,
>> that our Lord is greater than all gods.
> *The LORD does whatever pleases him,*
>> in the heavens and on the earth,
>> in the seas and all their depths. . . .

> The idols of the nations are silver and gold,
>     made by the hands of men. (Ps. 135:5–6, 15)

As Bolin rightly notes, the thematic and phraseological overlap between these passages and Jonah underscores the points made above: worshiping any other god besides Yahweh is futile. Moreover, his power stretches to every corner of creation; in the heavens and the earth, *the Lord does whatever pleases him.*

Now I do not think that the text warrants squeezing conversion stories out of the chapter at this point. Calvin says essentially the same when he explains the limitations of the concept of the fear of the Lord that our text says these sailors experienced. Even so, just as young children in dysfunctional homes learn survival strategies that are ingrained for years, and just as combat veterans have inculcated in their minds memories for a lifetime, so the sailors were caught up in a schoolhouse experience not of their own making and which could not easily be forgotten. Jack Sasson is worth quoting at length here:

> But the contest aboard the ship was no longer just between Jonah and his God. The sailors were discovering the hard way that the events aboard ship were by no means a drama about wayward individuals and divine vengeance; nor were they about testing human compassion under impossible circumstances. Rather, they were about learning a lesson wherever and whenever a prophet of God appeared— willingly or otherwise. The lesson itself is one that Israel has been taught repeatedly, but one that Israel must be made to recall throughout its history: that the God who apportions death can also grant life and that unconditional submission to divine will can, in fact, turn fate around. When learned under stressful

conditions, such difficult lessons are especially prone to longlasting retention.[5]

The sailors may not have converted, but certainly they are caught up in the drama of a prophet of the one true God which has left them indelibly changed. From their perspective they may have only been adding one more god to the pantheon of gods whom they venerated; however, the lessons learned undoubtedly would not be easily forgotten. Such facts should give Christians pause as we contemplate our role and potential impact in the world, for better or worse.

## PROPHET OVERBOARD: DEATH WISH OR HEROIC COMPASSION?

One of the major issues in this chapter is to determine whether Jonah's instructions to the sailors were noble or whether the instructions were merely a death wish on Jonah's part without any consideration of the sailors' well-being. Commentators on the biblical text are divided over the issue. More precisely, they land all over the map of possibilities.

The decision to go one way or another on this issue is often clouded by the fact that Jonah does seem to have a death wish in chapter 4. People often assume that his psychological state is the same here as in chapter 4. Another crucial question in chapter 1 is determining whether Jonah's attitude toward outsiders (Gentiles) here in this chapter is similar to, or different from, what we see reflected in chapter 4 of Jonah. In short, in chapter 1 is Jonah a "selfish xenophobe,"[6] or, "as the result of repentance and returning to duty, [is] Jonah's soul . . . placid, meek, and mild as a weaned child—calmly strong in righteousness"?[7]

In dealing with these questions, we must first admit that the author of Jonah has not given us a clue at this point in the story that would indicate clearly what was going on in Jonah's mind. By no means do we want to deny the possibility of discerning the author's intent, but the only access we have to that intent is what is written down before us. Unlike chapter 4, there are no cues here in chapter 1 to direct us to Jonah's thinking. Second, it is going beyond what is actually in the text to assume that Jonah's attitude toward the sailors here is the same as it is toward the Ninevites in chapter 4. The author simply does not tell us.

One would hope upon arriving at the prayer from the depths in chapter 2 that there would be more clarity rather than opaqueness with respect to Jonah's thinking. One would hope that the author might disambiguate Jonah's thought processes for us there. Rather, in chapter 2, the effect is a continuance of mounting dramatic tension that begins here in chapter 1. With respect to his posture toward the Gentiles, we must continue waiting. No immediate answer is given.

All of the above must be carefully held in mind if one is to avoid going beyond what the text actually does say. Consider, for example, the following statements by Edmund Clowney, which seem to say more than is actually warranted by the text:

> Jonah decided that he was expendable. God had called him to warn Nineveh that in forty days it would be destroyed. Suppose he removed himself from action: the Ninevites would not receive the warning, and Nineveh's destruction would be certain. Jonah was willing to perish so that Israel might be preserved. His decision explains not only his scheme to take a voyage, but also the remarkable calm that enabled him to sleep through the gale that soon swept over the ship. When his identity was disclosed to the terrified sailors, he offered a second

plan that seemed even more effective. Let them throw him overboard. The storm came from the Lord; Jonah was the object of God's wrath. Jonah would drown, the sailors would survive—and Nineveh would hear no warning.[8]

Where does the text indicate that this is why Jonah hatched this plan?

What can we say about Jonah's wish to be jettisoned like a piece of cargo, originally introduced in 1:12? It seems probable that Jonah did not want to go to Nineveh because going there would not bode well for Israel. To fulfill his commission and see the repentance of the Ninevites would entail judgment for Israel, Jonah's beloved fatherland. As Clowney has noted in discussion of the prophet's choice, "What if Nineveh repents of its wickedness? Will God spare it? If Nineveh is spared, how can Israel be safe?"[9] But we do not know if that was front and center in Jonah's thinking here. At the same time, we are justified in some other assumptions.

Given the word that Jonah uses to command the sailors (*nasa'*, "lift up"), Jack Sasson has described how Jonah's wish to be tossed overboard operates on different levels.[10] First, on the *narrative level*, the choice of words undergirds Jonah's control of the situation. Second, on the *psychological level*, we can say something about the sailors since the text itself gives us certain clues in this respect. The sailors are given pause by the radical nature of Jonah's command. They are actually commanded to pick him up and throw him overboard! Although we may not, on the basis of the text, say anything about Jonah's psychological motivation at this point, we may say something about the sailors' psychological hesitation. Third, at the *semantic level*, it is at least interesting to note that the verb used by Jonah is often used of the removal of sin, but only rarely is it used in the manner that Jonah uses it. This too may be suggestive.

So we return to our previous questions. Was Jonah's command a heroic one or a death wish on Jonah's part? The very structure of this question destroys the balance of a middle way, namely, that what Jonah tells the sailors to do in verse 12 "is neither Jonah's final solution to evade his mission . . . nor a gallant bid of vicarious sacrifice."[11] But certainly from the perspective of the sailors we may say that the text leaves open the possibility that Jonah's command could be considered an "oblative act of generosity."[12] Calvin goes so far as to call it expiation. Consequently, it is both a death wish and, insofar as the action succeeds in rescuing the lives of the sailors, then we may say in hindsight that it is also a heroic act whether a noble motivation or a perverted plan was central in Jonah's thought processes, which we do not know.

Now, having dealt with the immediate horizon of Jonah's experience, we may ask how this episode fits into the larger canonical context. Although I disagree with some of Jacques Ellul's thoughtful book, he does, in my opinion, correctly recognize an illustration of Christ in the section under discussion. I quote for the reader part of what he states:

> At this point [in chapter 1] Jonah takes up the role of the scapegoat. And the sacrifice he makes saves [the sailors]. The sea calms down. He saves them humanly and materially. They will not be drowned because of his fault. . . . What counts is that this story is in reality the precise intimation of an infinitely vaster story and one which concerns us directly. What Jonah could not do, but his attitude announces, is done by Jesus Christ. He it is who accepts total condemnation. . . . It is solely because of the sacrifice of Jesus Christ that the sacrifice of

Jonah avails and saves. It is solely because Jesus Christ has accepted malediction that Jonah's acceptance has something to say both to the sailors and to us.[13]

An even fuller quotation from Ellul would need more qualification (since he sees Jonah as "saving" the sailors spiritually as well). However, in general terms, he got it right.

Let the reader remember that there are many differences between Jonah and Christ that must be kept in mind (see p. 44). Certainly the New Testament affirms that this is "a trustworthy saying that deserves full acceptance: Christ Jesus came into the world to save sinners—of whom I am the worst. . . . For there is one God and one mediator between God and men, the man Christ Jesus, who gave himself as a ransom for all men—the testimony given in its proper time" (1 Tim. 1:15; 2:5–6). Jesus Christ, the Son of man, gave his life as a ransom for many. Jonah could not give his life for the sins of the sailors; only the sinless Jesus Christ could fulfill that role in an eternal sense. Here the disparity between Christ and Jonah could not be more apparent. The sacrifice of Christ is clearer and greater than the opaqueness of Jonah's relatively meager expiation.

The sailors did as the man of God had told them to do, and the outcome was exactly as the man of God said it would be: the sea ceased from its rage, another strange personification almost completely lost on modern readers. And so the sailors not only feared (vv. 5, 10) a great fear (v. 10), but they feared a great fear and they feared the Lord, and once again the name of the Hebrew God is used (v. 16)! The author has carefully woven an escalating use of fear into the passage. But the sailors will live and so too will Jonah (unbeknownst to them).

# FOR FURTHER REFLECTION

1. What two literary devices were discussed in this chapter? Can you identify and define them?
2. What is the relationship between structure and meaning?
3. What is the mood aboard this ship destined for Tarshish?
4. What role did lot-casting play in the narrative of chapter 1?
5. Is there a change in the characterization of the sailors in chapter 1?
6. What is Jonah's motive in asking the sailors to throw him overboard?

# 5

## INTO THE FISH'S BELLY (1:17)

And this is the tragedy of the Book of Jonah, that a
Book which is made the means of one of the most sublime revelations of truth in the Old Testament should be
known to most only for its connections with a whale.
(G. A. Smith, quoted by Rosemary Nixon)[1]

Again: as the profound calm which only apparently pre-
cedes and prophesies of the storm, is perhaps more
awful than the storm itself; for, indeed, the calm is but
the wrapper and envelope of the storm; and contains it
in itself, as the seemingly harmless rifle holds the fatal
powder, and the ball and the explosion; so the graceful
repose of the line, as it silently serpentines about the
oarsmen before being brought into play—this is a thing
which carries more of true terror than any other aspect
of this dangerous affair [whaling]. But why say more?
All men live enveloped in whale-lines. All are born with
halters round their necks; but it is only when caught in
the swift, sudden turn of death, that mortals realize the
silent, subtle, ever-present perils of life. (Herman
Melville, *Moby Dick*)

> But the LORD provided a great fish to swallow Jonah, and Jonah was inside the fish three days and three nights. (Jonah 1:17)

As Jonah predicted, the sea became calm as the sailors lifted him overboard (1:12, 15). While the sailors breathed relief above deck, Jonah's life hung in the balance in the water below.

But God had not forgotten him.

It's important for us to talk briefly about chapter divisions in the Bible before continuing. The reader should remember that chapter divisions and versification of the Bible have not always been part of the text of Scripture. These additions were inserted in the medieval period to enhance clarification of Scripture. With regard to the chapter divisions in Jonah, it makes a difference whether one reads the text in Hebrew or English. The standard Hebrew text places the verse that describes the whale swallowing Jonah in the first verse of chapter 2. The NIV on the other hand (with most other Protestant editions) places this verse at the end of chapter 1 (thus, v. 17).

This is significant. For if the verse in question is presented as occurring at the beginning of chapter 2, then it has the effect of sounding like a new development in the plot and therefore introducing Jonah's poem from the deep. Consequently, the swallowing of Jonah and the poem of chapter 2 (vv. 2–9 in English) have integrity. That is to say, they hang together. The poem in chapter 2 is bound together with the verse describing Jonah being swallowed by the big fish.

But if the verse is retained in chapter 1 as verse 17 (as it is in the NIV), then the effect is different: the verse recalls actions occurring on board the ship. Jonah is thrown overboard, the sea grows calm, and the sailors worship the one true God while Jonah disappears down the gullet of a huge fish. How long did the fish take to show up? The fact of the matter is that the text simply does not say. Ancient versions indicate that the translators wrestled with this issue in various ways and supplied different answers.

We are now approaching what is arguably one of the most well known sections of Scripture: Jonah in the belly of the fish. Before we deal with the sublime poem, however, there are some preliminary points that need to be made in order to lay the groundwork for our discussion of Jonah in the belly of the fish.

Many perplexing issues are raised in this section of Jonah. Why is chapter 2 in poetry and not prose? Was this poem a later addition to the prose sections? Why is there a prayer of thanksgiving issuing from the belly of the fish as opposed to a confession of sin and petition for pardon as we would expect? What is the role of the fish in this passage? Does Jonah in the belly of the fish represent Israel, Israel in exile, every person? In what sense? More importantly still, how exactly does Christ our Lord compare himself with Jonah? Before addressing these questions we need to discuss the exact function of the big fish.

## THE FUNCTION OF THE FISH

What role the fish plays in this section is crucial to the overall understanding of the immediate passage and the book as a whole. Was the fish appointed by God to rescue Jonah prior to and without reference to Jonah's psalm, or was the giant fish given as a response to Jonah's prayer? Was the fish a rescue or a punishment? These kinds of questions have led to a division of interpretation on this significant section of the book.

In fact, wrestling over the exact role of the fish is crucial to understanding the psalm of Jonah. It is interesting to note, as some commentators have, that God's appointing the fish in 1:17 and commanding the fish in 2:10 provide a framing device by which God's control of the situation is made a primary focus.[2]

In short, it seems that the author of Jonah has God intending the fish to rescue Jonah. The fish is not a means of punishment but of snatching from drowning. Jonah is saved in spite of his recalcitrance, and thus he experiences the pity and mercy of God. Hence the climactic exultation "Salvation comes from the LORD" (2:9) is a fitting conclusion to the psalm. This interpretation is supported by the fact that the Hebrew verb used to describe "swallowing" does not have the negative connotation that it usually does (cf. Isa. 28:4 with Num. 16:31–34 and Prov. 1:12). In this passage, the fish's swallowing is a means of deliverance; indeed, there may be irony present here.

God appoints the fish in order to rescue Jonah, but God also appoints the fish for pedagogical reasons as well; in fact, Jonah has lessons to learn. This can be determined not only from the general context but also from a close study of the opening verb of verse 17 (2:1 in Hebrew). This verb, *minnah* (piel), occurs several times in the book of Jonah (1:17; 4:6, 7, 8). Jack Sasson's analysis has shown that three things happen with each occurrence of this word in Jonah: a different name for God is used; the object of control following the verb belongs to a different order of nature; and there is a pun.

After looking both inside and outside the book of Jonah at the nuances conveyed by this verb and the words that are associated with it, Sasson makes a significant point: "*minnâ*, [piel: "appoint"] is an act that generally needs a medium through which to be fulfilled."[3] Applying this to the material at hand, Sasson concludes that God is keen to produce the most "appropriate conditions for teaching Jonah the desired lessons."[4] Jonah's temporary quarters in the belly of this large fish provide just the right context for him to learn something about himself and God. Whether or not the lesson had the intended effect on Jonah is another matter, one that will become evident in the course of the continuing story.

## LESSONS ON TYPOLOGY

Now is a good time for us to examine a very important kind of interpretation that often occurs in Scripture. Sometimes individuals are used in Scripture as types of Christ (e.g., David, Jonah, Solomon, Elijah). Sometimes events, experiences, or institutions are used as types and find their fulfillment in Christ. For example, the New Testament understands Israel to be a type of the church (Gal. 6:16; James 1:1; Rev. 21:12–14).

Generally, although typological interpretation has fallen on hard times recently, scholars can agree on the following definition: "Typological interpretation of the Old Testament is based on the 'presupposition that the whole Old Testament looks beyond itself for its interpretation.' Historically this meant that 'types and prophecies of the coming Christ were sought throughout the Old Testament, and with the life of Christ already known to all, they were readily found.' "[5] For example, David as the king of Israel was a shadowy type of Christ, who would become the ultimate fulfillment of the Old Testament office of king.

Typology is a method of biblical interpretation that has a time-honored pedigree and was practiced by such luminaries in the past as John Calvin, Martin Luther, Geerhardus Vos, and many others. The underlying principle behind typological interpretation is that God acts in a constant manner. Typological interpretation demonstrates that Old Testament events, individuals, and institutions (the types) looked beyond themselves for their ultimate fulfillment and interpretation in the antitype (i.e., the thing typified). In other words, the Old Testament types prefigured in shadowy form things to come (the antitype). For example, Adam, as a type portrayed in the Old Testament, prefigured Christ (the last Adam), the antitype who came in the fullness of time.

Some Old Testament scholars have argued that one of Israel's foundational and fundamental concerns—a primary preoccupation involving even their understanding of life—was the "typical occurrence [i.e., typological occurrences]."[6] Moreover, our Lord himself understood the Old Testament typologically. For example, he understood Jonah as a type of himself. Furthermore, recent studies in the philosophy of language have confirmed the validity of typology as a method for understanding biblical literature. Therefore, it behooves us to define our terms and clarify our methods carefully if we are to understand this kind of interpretation and discuss its application to the book of Jonah.

Typology is used in various ways in biblical studies. Some people use it in a mere literary sense. For example, since Jacob goes through a tremendous transformation of character in the patriarchal narratives, he becomes a symbol exploited by the later prophets in order to encourage exiled Hebrews that God can overcome the enemies who threaten them. Somewhat similarly, some use typological interpretation to describe how later Israelites reinterpreted their past, using old paradigms and symbols in new ways to justify or give meaning to present events. Still others have seen typological interpretation as rooted in historical events of the past which were ordained by God's sovereignty in preparation for a heightened or at least fuller expression of the truth, which has now been realized in the coming of Christ.

That Jesus Christ drew an analogy between himself and Jonah is impossible to deny (Matt. 12:39–40). What the exact nature of that analogy was and how it informs the way in which we read the Old Testament not only at this point but elsewhere need clarification.

Some suggest that there must always be some kind of heightening between the type and the antitype (e.g., Jesus is a greater king than David). Others suggest that this "increase" simply flows naturally from the relationship between the Old Testament and the New Testament: there is progression from the type to the antitype. Most agree—but not all—that typological interpretation as developed by the Reformers and their heirs differs from allegorical interpretation (James Barr is a notable exception).[7]

Still others use typology in a sense very similar to allegory so that it becomes difficult if not impossible to distinguish between the two. This should not be the case. In allegorical interpretation, the literal sense (not to be confused with the *literalistic* interpretation) is dismissed and history takes a back seat, so to speak. Individual parts of the story are interpreted through allegorical lenses so that, for example, the flight of rebellious Jonah symbolizes Israel's failure as a whole to fulfill her purpose of mission to the surrounding nations. Overinterpreting the role of the fish has also led many writers into unwarranted allegorical interpretations of this section of Scripture.

Indeed, there are allegories in the Bible (e.g., Gal. 4); however, I am presently discussing the allegorical method of interpretation, not allegorical texts. Allegorical interpretations attempt to find a deeper and more profound meaning in the text than is warranted. Kevin Vanhoozer sums up the difference well: "The crucial difference between figural or typological interpretation and its allegorical counterpart is that the former relates two items that stand in a historical relation of anticipation and fulfillment, whereas no such relation regulates the connection between the literal and spiritual senses in allegory."[8]

Jonah 1:17 is a good example of how some interpret Jonah in an allegorical sense. In Jonah 1:17 Jonah is swallowed up. On the backside of the poem (2:10), Jonah is vomited out. These verses frame the poem and Jonah's experience in the belly of the large fish. Commentators have noted this language of being swallowed and subsequently disgorged in other parts of the Old Testament, especially in Leviticus 18:24–28 and Jeremiah 51:34. In Leviticus 18, the Israelites are warned that if they transgress God's law and defile the land, the land will vomit them out. In Jeremiah 51:34, the prophet laments Israel's being swallowed up in exile by the ruler of Babylon, Nebuchadnezzar:

> Nebuchadnezzar king of Babylon has devoured us,
>> he has thrown us into confusion,
>> he has made us an empty jar.
> Like a serpent [*tannin*] he has swallowed us
>> and filled his stomach with our delicacies,
>> and then has spewed us out.

At first glance this apparently remarkable correspondence may prove too appealing to pass up, especially if we see Jonah as representing Israel in some sense as we suggested above in chapter 2. In fact many have not passed it by and have used Jeremiah 51:34 in support of an allegorical interpretation. Indeed, in the 1800s one writer, interpreting the text of Jonah allegorically, asserted that the fish is Babylon, Jonah is Israel, and the booth in chapter 4 is the restoration of Jerusalem after the exile.[9] A number of writers since then have followed suit, asserting that Jonah's aquatic adventure is a picture of Israel in exile.

But in spite of the fact that some of the imagery is similar at first glance, a more careful reading should give the interpreter pause before diving into the allegorical method. Such an interpretation is strained, in my opinion, and fails to understand the text. First, note on the conceptual level that the function of the fish in Jonah is to deliver Jonah safe to dry ground, not to punish him. In other words, the function of the fish in the book of

Jonah is the opposite of the function in the passages appealed to by those who argue for an allegorical interpretation of Jonah 1:17.

Second, the word used to portray the fish (*dag*) in Jonah is different from the word used of Nebuchadnezzar (*tannin*, "sea serpent"). Some will object that I am being what might be called an "exegetical allusion or citation policeman" and imposing too rigorous restrictions on biblical allusions (e.g., that allusions can occur only when there is exact citation of words and not images). Inner-biblical interpretation and allusions by biblical writers are common occurrences and more complex than space allows for discussion here. However, for the reasons stated above, Jonah 1:17 (and chapter 2 which follows) should probably not be interpreted as a picture of Israel in exile. But if we turn to the New Testament for an understanding of Jonah and inner-biblical interpretation, we find firm grounding in our Lord's own exegesis of the passage.

## THE SIGN OF JONAH:
## OLD TESTAMENT TYPOLOGY IN
## THE LIGHT OF THE NEW TESTAMENT

Jonah is perhaps one of the most significant examples of an Old Testament individual serving as a type of Jesus. This assumes, of course, that the passage in Matthew 12:40 is authentic, a position adopted in this book.[10] There are many references in the Gospels where our Lord looks back to Jonah (Matt. 12:38–42; 16:4; Luke 11:29–30, 32). However, the passage from Matthew 12 is the most helpful for our purposes:

> Then some of the Pharisees and teachers of the law said to him, "Teacher, we want to see a miraculous sign from you."

He answered, "A wicked and adulterous generation asks for a miraculous sign! But none will be given it except the sign of the prophet Jonah. For as Jonah was three days and three nights in the belly of a huge fish, so the Son of Man will be three days and three nights in the heart of the earth. The men of Nineveh will stand up at the judgment with this generation and condemn it; for they repented at the preaching of Jonah, and now one greater than Jonah is here. The Queen of the South will rise at the judgment with this generation and condemn it; for she came from the ends of the earth to listen to Solomon's wisdom, and now one greater than Solomon is here."

In this passage, Jesus refers to Jonah as a type of himself. Clearly, certain correspondences between Jonah and Jesus are being made, but in what sense?[11]

Note that Jesus compares himself with Jonah in two respects: Jonah was entombed in the belly of the fish (v. 40a), and so Jesus will be entombed (v. 40b) in the heart of the earth; and just as Jonah was a preacher of repentance to Nineveh, so one greater than Jonah has come preaching repentance as well, namely Jesus Christ. As Jonah and his preaching were a sign to the Ninevites, so Jesus and his preaching are a sign to the present generation.

Likewise, just as Jonah's preaching was validated by the miraculous deliverance from the fish, so too Jesus' preaching and mission will be validated by a miraculous deliverance, in this case the resurrection. Our Lord's preaching at this point is made with forceful application: the present generation (in this case the Pharisees and teachers of the law are in the gallery) should repent even as the Ninevites did because someone greater than Jonah is addressing them! Jesus is a greater prophet than Jonah because the fulfillment of all that Jonah and his mission foreshadowed is now being realized on a higher level.

Now Matthew moves on to a comparison with Solomon in 12:42. An appeal to Wisdom is in the background. Although the comparison is moving beyond Jonah here, the typological interpretation (foreshadowing and fulfillment) is instructive for our purposes again. If Gentiles (the Queen of the South in this case) responded to Solomon's wisdom, how much more so should those who hear Jesus' words respond since someone greater than Solomon is here!

A prophet and a king have been superseded, both titles and offices which Christ has filled in a greater way than Jonah or Solomon ever could. The present generation would do well to take notice lest their guilt be justly condemned for falling short even of those pagans (the Ninevites and the Queen of the South) who heard and witnessed the type, not the antitype!

If one takes the entire twelfth chapter of Matthew into consideration, then the fulfillment theme becomes even more pronounced. In 12:3–6, the relationship between Jesus and David is established. Verse 6 "makes explicit the basic assumption that 'something greater is here.' "[12] When one realizes that throughout Matthew 12 Jesus' authority is being established vis-à-vis the Pharisees on the basis of his fulfillment of the Old Testament, what is especially remarkable is the Old Testament figures that were chosen for establishing Jesus' credentials. R. T. France comments:

> The Old Testament "models" selected add up to a remarkable overview of the main channels through which God's authority was formerly exercised among his people—David, the greatest king (and model of messianic expectation), the temple and its priesthood, Jonah as a representative prophet, and Solomon the wise man (and also, the king, the son of David). To have claimed that in Jesus all these lines of authority came together and found their contemporary mani-

festation would have been bold enough. But he is "greater," "more" than all of them.[13]

France sums up his treatment of Old Testament typology very neatly when he writes about Christ fulfilling the Old Testament:

> In all these aspects of the Old Testament people of God Jesus sees foreshadowings of himself and his work, with its results in the opposition and consequent rejection of the majority of the Jews, while the true Israel is now to be found in the new Christian community. Thus in his coming the history of Israel has reached its decisive point. The whole of the Old Testament is gathered up in him. He himself embodies in his own person the status and destiny of Israel, and in the community of those who belong to him that status and destiny are to be fulfilled, no longer in the nation as such.[14]

Although God spoke through many voices and through many different and distinct kinds of literature in the Old Testament, the Scriptures showcase a marvelous unfolding unity and continuity. A judicious use of the typological method of interpretation, far from pointing to a disorganization or confusion in the Scriptures, actually emphasizes the continuity and fulfillment of Scripture that climax in the person and work of Christ. Preachers who would use the typological method responsibly are doing a great service for the saints who are given into their care.

## A SONG OF "SILENCE"

When the reader comes to the beginning of the psalm in Jonah, the action slows down and almost comes to a standstill. Was the fish there to swallow Jonah as soon as he hit the water, or was the prophet left flapping around in the water for a time? The ancient versions that translated the verse dealt with this question in different ways; however, the Hebrew text doesn't tell us one way or another, nor is it really important for the meaning. In the Hebrew text there is a strong pausal accent (*atnach*) right in the middle of the verse, "But the Lord provided a great fish to swallow Jonah . . . ," and this may have signaled a slowing down of the reading. Beyond this, the text says nothing. This deliberate pause supports the gist of the author's upcoming point.

Perhaps nothing has captured the mood any better than the deft pen of Sasson: "In this chapter, once Jonah plunges into the waters, further events turn strangely limp, with only the novelty of an enwombed human to occupy an audience's attention and to stir its curiosity. The action is about to come to a full halt in order to leave Jonah alone with his God."[15] In the silence, there is a sense in which we too are dragged beneath the surface of the water, uncertain and holding our breath for what will happen next. Although I previously demurred from the position that Jonah somehow represents "every person," nevertheless, in chapter 2 the author draws us into a sympathetic reading of Jonah by his intense engagement with the emotions and cries of the drowning, dying man. Jonah, on the brink of death, is about to experience a profound encounter with the living God.

The question occurs, What would our last thoughts be if we knew we were soon going to die and go out into eternity? We should be challenged as we read the psalm of Jonah. If we are honest, we often live at a hectic velocity. This fast pace, many times marked by our own secret rebellion, means we have no time for stillness of soul, for solitude to examine who we really are and what we have or haven't done. As one commentator has adroitly said: "Here lies the secret of the book's continuing fascination, for readers see an aspect of self in its compelling story. What one makes of it will depend partly on self-understanding and partly on one's grasp of the all-embracing love of the God we serve."[16]

Chapter 2 of Jonah should haunt us and shake us out of our own doldrums because we are so often just like Jonah. It should also encourage us because Jonah experiences the mercy of God and declares in thankfulness, "Salvation comes from the LORD" (2:9).

## FOR FURTHER REFLECTION

1. What is the function of the fish in Jonah?
2. What lessons can be learned about God's character from his sending the fish to rescue Jonah?
3. What is the difference between allegory and typology? Give an example of both.
4. How is Jesus like Jonah? How is he unlike Jonah?
6. What role does God's mercy play in this part of the book?

# 6

## PRAYER FROM THE DEPTHS:
## PART 1 (2:1–6a)

Although to the healthy and pure internal eye He [Christ] is everywhere present, He saw fit to appear to those whose eye is weak and impure, and even to fleshly eyes. (Augustine, *On Christian Doctrine*)

From inside the fish Jonah prayed to the LORD his God. He said: "In my distress I called to the LORD, and he answered me. From the depths of the grave I called for help, and you listened to my cry. You hurled me into the deep, into the very heart of the seas, and the currents swirled about me; all your waves and breakers swept over me. I said, 'I have been banished from your sight; yet I will look again toward your holy temple.' The engulfing waters threatened me, the deep surrounded me; seaweed was wrapped around my head. To the roots of the mountains I sank down; the earth beneath barred me in forever." (Jonah 2:1–6a)

# JONAH'S DESCENT: A WATERY GRAVE?

In the previous chapter, we saw how our Lord compared himself with Jonah. Just as Jonah was entombed within the fish, so also Jesus was entombed in the grave. But the story did not end there. Just as Jonah was delivered safe from his watery grave, so also Christ Jesus emerged victorious from the grave. Jonah's passage through death and coming out alive is an image of Christ's ultimate victory over the grave when he himself is raised from the dead. The type (Jonah) is now seen more clearly in the antitype (Christ). Now that the shadow is made manifest in the reality, we are prepared to read the details of the poem in chapter 2 and observe more precisely just how Jonah's watery ordeal illustrates Christ's death and resurrection.

At the end of the previous chapter, we also commented on how the poem in chapter 2 of Jonah has the effect of retarding and suspending the action. Everything slows. Accordingly, the reader is brought to a full stop. This is a reflective dirge.

Jonah's descent has hit rock bottom here in verse 6 of chapter 2, "To the roots of the mountains I sank down [*yaradti*]." Jonah is closer to death than life in this psalm. I say this not only because Jonah is drowning, but also because death in the Old Testament is more than the physical cessation of life. Death is not limited to merely that point in time when the brain and heart cease to function. This is not to deny that death is physical, but to assert that it is more than that. Since the fall of mankind, the power and influence of death have permeated our whole existence, a fact of which we are acutely aware whenever we suffer. So then, life in the Old Testament means more than a beating heart; life is better described as fullness of life (a robust life), something compromised by the shadow of death. Life and death are in constant tension.

It may be startling to the reader that Jonah's encounter with death occurs in a section of poetry sandwiched between two chapters of prose. However, the Old Testament often mixes prose and poetry. Sometimes the Hebrew Bible breaks into poetry right in the middle of prose (e.g., Ex. 15; Num. 23–24; Judg. 5). Interestingly, some of the oldest poetry in the Bible is found exactly at these junctures.

Jonah 2:2–9 is recognized universally as transitioning from Hebrew prose to poetry. There is, then, a departure from the normal constraints of prose, and the language shifts to reflect the characteristics of Hebrew poetry.

In the twentieth century, many Bible scholars thought that the psalm located in Jonah 2 didn't belong to the original composition. They thought that the poem lacked integrity with the prose sections coming before and after, and concluded that it was probably written by a different hand and inserted into the book at a later time. Other scholars asserted that the poetry came first and the prose sections were added later. Recent trends have shown a more cautious approach, however.

George Landes, for example, has argued strongly for a contextual interpretation of the psalm.[1] Since his work appeared, many others have followed suit, arguing for the integrity of the poem within the narrative. Although the psalm may have existed independently at some point, it probably had found its place within the text by the time that the overall book of Jonah first appeared. It is noteworthy that the psalm is located in the same position in the Dead Sea Scrolls, our earliest manuscript witness to the text of Jonah. Recent studies have demonstrated that the "text of [Jonah 2:2–9] is neither an idle copy nor a lazy crib; it was placed where it is with deliberation; it did not fall accidentally into a gap in some scribe's attention."[2]

There are two points that I wish to make about the poetry of this chapter: it is highly stylized and it is thoroughly aquatic. First, the poem is a sublime piece of work representing the highest level of organizational achievement and artifice. It is replete with images and motifs that were commonplace in the world of the ancient Hebrew. Far from being a mere pastiche or hodgepodge of images sloppily cut-and-pasted from a variety of other sources, or merely an attempt to imitate a more pristine piece of poetry with some kind of literary pretense, the poem itself is a stylized hymn of individual thanksgiving demonstrating the highest level of artistic achievement.

The prayer that is articulated in chapter 2, as Uriel Simon asserts, can be apprehended correctly only if the reader understands that it does not follow the expected chronological sequence (distress—prayer—response—thanksgiving).[3] That is to say, chapter 2 begins, in typical Hebrew fashion, by giving the bottom line (v. 1, "From inside the fish Jonah prayed") and then proceeds to give the details of that prayer. The interweaving of themes in these verses (especially the prophet's distress, his prayer, and God's response) and the chiastic structure demonstrate that we are dealing with more than mere chronological sequence here.

Our discussion of the first chapter of Jonah mentioned a literary technique that the ancients sometimes used called chiasm. Although I questioned whether this introverted structure actually appears in chapter 1, the poetry of chapter 2 is full of chiastic structures on both a large and small scale.[4] A detailed discussion of the poetic structure of Jonah 2 is beyond the scope of this book. Even so, in order that the reader may appreciate some of the artistic form that can be found in this poem, take note of the striking chiastic arrangement:

A *Underworld*
(v. 2)

In my distress I called to the LORD,
   and he answered me.
From the depths of the grave I called for help
   [literally, from the belly of Sheol],
   and you listened to my cry.

| B | *Cosmic waters* (v. 3) | You hurled me into the deep,<br>    into the very heart of the seas,<br>    and the currents swirled about me;<br>all your waves and breakers<br>    swept over me. |
|---|---|---|
| C | *Poet's plight* (v. 4) | I said, "I have been banished<br>    from your sight;<br>yet I will look again<br>    toward your holy temple." |
| B′ | *Cosmic waters* (v. 5) | The engulfing waters threatened me,<br>    the deep surrounded me;<br>    seaweed was wrapped around my head. |
| A′ | *Underworld* (v. 6) | To the roots of the mountains I sank down;<br>    the earth beneath barred me in forever. |

As Frank Moore Cross has noted, "this is an exquisite example of cyclic construction."[5] There are even more detailed and ornate structures that space limitations do not allow me to discuss. Note that the center of the chiasm (v. 4) characterizes the poet's plight. The affirmation of trust and resolve, so characteristic of psalms of thanksgiving, does not come until the end (v. 9, which will be discussed in the next chapter).

Not only is the poem the product of a gifted poet, it is also an example of a psalm brimming with water imagery; stated simply, it is aquatic. Many psalms in the Bible contain allusions to water and drowning in order to convey a feeling of severe distress. Consider some verses from Psalm 69:

Save me, O God,
    for the waters have come up to my neck.
I sink in the miry depths,
    where there is no foothold.
I have come into the deep waters;
    the floods engulf me. (vv. 1–2)

Rescue me from the mire,
    do not let me sink;

> deliver me from those who hate me,
>     from the deep waters.
> Do not let the floodwaters engulf me
>     or the depths swallow me up
>     or the pit close its mouth over me. (vv. 14–15)

Although it may not be immediately evident to the modern reader, the Psalms mix water imagery with imagery from the underworld as well as with various names for the underworld such as "the pit," "Abaddon," or "Sheol." These images and synonyms are very common in the psalm of Jonah. Water and pit imagery are found in four of the seven verses of this poem. As one author has remarked, "The most concentrated water and pit imagery of the Psalter . . . is not nearly as concentrated as that. . . . We may say then, to hazard a pun, that this short psalm releases a veritable flood of water imagery."[6]

The NIV translates verse 2b, "From the depths of the grave I called for help," but the Hebrew actually says, "From the *belly of Sheol* I cried out." As Jack Sasson says, the metaphor "is unique to Jonah and conveys despair of the darkest hue."[7] Before we explore the meaning of the water imagery and the imagery associated with Sheol, we must unpack the meaning of this concept that is often alluded to in the Psalms. What significance does this place called Sheol have for the Old Testament saint? As a matter of fact, death, the afterlife, and Sheol have been the subject of much discussion in recent years.[8]

In the majority of Old Testament references, Sheol is used to describe human fate. It is a place to which one does not want to go, an "unwelcome fate." Sheol refers to a place of divine punishment, a curse often wished on the ungodly. Thanks to recent discoveries of texts from the ancient Near East, we now understand better the imagery of Sheol and the underworld.

Sometimes in the ancient Near East we find the imagery of entering the mouth of Death itself (*Mot*). Stories were told of the battles between order and chaotic forces—including water—in the great cosmological war, which was between life and death. Frequently the battle was between the sea and some other deity or imaginary god, whether that god was something like a king (Marduk) or Death personified (*Mot*). This mythology is taken up and used in a conflation of images in the Psalms and here in Jonah 2 as well. Jonah turns to this realm of chaos and primitive battling of primeval forces in order to articulate his feelings of despair and suffering. Human language is strained to the utter breaking point to adequately encompass the suffering Jonah has to endure at this point.

Jonah turns to the realm of death and chaos in order to express his anguish. Clearly Sheol here is used in a metaphorical manner since Jonah is still alive and is offering up this prayer. He is using language to describe an existence already in the realm of Sheol, albeit he is near drowning as well. But not only does Jonah employ language from the realm of death and Sheol, he also turns to another particular stock of images: cosmological battle. The anguished voice of Jonah in this psalm is like one engaged in the ancient mythical battle with chaos.

Jonah cries out from his watery grave in very direct address, "*You* hurled me into the deep, into the very heart of the seas, and the currents swirled about me; all *your* waves and breakers swept over me" (v. 3). Although the sailors actually jettisoned Jonah overboard, Jonah recognized that it was God who was the ultimate originator of the action.

Jonah desperately gropes for the right words to express his extreme near-drowning distress. As Philip Johnston has stated, "Sheol is at the opposite theological extreme to Yahweh, and the dominant feature for its inhabitants is their separation from him."[9] Jonah senses that he is abandoned by God and uses the common motifs at his disposal to express his grief. In other words, Jonah is straining to the uttermost to find language to accurately express his despair.

Whatever the inestimable grief that Jonah feels in his cry at this point, there is another who entered into a state of forsakenness beyond anything ever imagined by human beings: total abandonment by God. Jonah got himself into trouble; Christ, on the other hand, accepted the wrath of God not to atone for his own shortcomings, but to pay the penalty for sins not his own. Christ cried out with a cry of dereliction never before imagined or equaled since. The expression of grief voiced by the strained human poem of Jonah finds its ultimate echo in Christ's cry from the cross.

## JESUS IN THE REALM OF DEATH

At the sixth hour darkness came over the whole land until the ninth hour. And at the ninth hour Jesus cried out in a loud voice, *"Eloi, Eloi, lama sabachthani?"*—which means, "My God, my God, why have you forsaken me?" (Mark 15:33–34)

Jesus Christ underwent abandonment of his own accord, not for his own sins and rebellion (like Jonah). He died for the sake of sinful creatures whom he came to redeem. Jesus bore God's wrath. Jonah experienced rescue from the ultimate abandonment, death itself. For Christ there was to be no immediate rescue and no respite. He would drink the cup of wrath to the dregs. Jesus' death would be much more than a mere physical death, although it was that. In order to understand the abandonment that Christ experienced, one needs to examine Christ's prayer in the garden of Gethsemane and the ordeal he experienced on Golgotha.

In the garden of Gethsemane, as Christ was preparing for his ordeal, our Lord said to his disciples, "My soul is overwhelmed with sorrow to the point of death. . . . Stay here and watch" (Mark 14:34). Then, a little later, he said in prayer to his Father in heaven, "*Abba*, Father . . . everything is possible for you. Take this cup from me. Yet not what I will, but what you will" (Mark 14:36). Now this cup metaphor is usually taken as no more than a metaphor for suffering; on the contrary, it is much more than that. In the Old Testament, the metaphorical use of cup often refers to God's punishment for sin. This cup is the cup of God's wrath against sin. Why did Christ not want to partake of this cup? It meant being utterly forsaken by God.

For Christ this forsakenness had at least three aspects.[10] First, abandonment by God meant withdrawal of all the creaturely comforts that we as human beings usually experience. Think about it. For Christ the sun was gone and only darkness was left. For Christ his honor had been put to shame (2 Cor. 8:9; Phil. 2:5–8). There was no comeliness about him as he was crucified (Isa. 53). For Christ there was no angel to support him in his darkest hour.[11]

Second, this abandonment for Christ was the experience of an active wrath exerted upon him by his heavenly Father. God the Father was sending all the torments of hell against the Son. As Klaas Schilder says, it is as if he were in the arena, like the martyrs of old, watching the animals being released one by one to tear at his flesh and crush his bones. And throughout the process, he saw his heavenly Father releasing the wrath against him, all the storehouses of wrath.[12]

Third, this was a veritable descent into hell for our Savior. Christ had to be identified with mankind in every respect, including the full experience of death itself: this was hell. He went through hell, so to speak, for a heavenly cause. This was separation from God himself, and what Christ had to experience.

The apostle Paul caught the great mystery when he said:

God made him who had no sin to be sin for us, so that in him we might become the righteousness of God. (2 Cor. 5:21)

Christ redeemed us from the curse of the law by becoming a curse for us, for it is written: "Cursed is everyone who is hung on a tree." (Gal. 3:13)

Together with John Calvin and others we may see in Christ's cry of derelliction, "My God, my God, why have you forsaken me?" the very finest commentary on the ancient creed, "He descended into hell." For it was not a literal hell into which he descended; it was the experience of hell as it is known in God-forsakenness.

This reflection, into which the psalm of Jonah has cast us, has to do with the subject of abandonment. As such it leaves us on the fringes of very great and profound mystery. Although Jesus was forsaken, the Father and the Holy Spirit were no mere spectators at the crucifixion. In Hebrews 9:14, for example, we read "through the eternal Spirit [he] offered himself unblemished to God." The "eternal Spirit" is undoubtedly the Holy Spirit. Moreover, in 2 Corinthians 5:18–19, we read "all this is from God, who reconciled us to himself through Christ. . . . God was reconciling the world to himself in Christ."

In this chapter we have talked much about death, suffering, and abandonment: Jonah's own suffering and as an image of Christ, the one greater than Jonah. We have also ventured the suggestion that in Jonah we see—especially in chapter 2—our own image in the wayward and suffering prophet. So how is one to respond to this dark psalm of Jonah's, which finds its ultimate echo in the cry of derelliction, that is, abandonment, uttered from the cross by our Savior in his darkest hour? That is to say, how should we apply this particular portion of God's Word to ourselves? We long to apply the message of God's Word. This is a natural response fueled by a desire to please God (usually). The Scripture must be *appropriately* applied. Such application will entail a great deal of work so that we protect ourselves and others from misapplying the Scriptures in a manner that is overly facile or simply moralistic.

Although there is something deep within our fallen nature that longs for moral imperatives and directives, the guidance of Scripture will frequently be more indirect than direct. Let me explain. There will not always be a tidy list of "dos" and "do nots" for us to follow. On the contrary. By way of example, missionary zeal may pour forth from a right application of the Psalms' overpowering message of the majesty of God rather than from a direct command to go out and disciple the nations such as is found at the end of the Gospels.[13] An appropriate application of the Psalms will often leave the audience with an intense adoration, marked by reverence and awe, at the fresh realization of knowing before whom they stand. Accordingly, inaction will not be the consequence of showcasing the glories of the Savior in the Scriptures; quite the contrary!

In Christ's suffering we find consolation for our trials, temptations, and rebellions. Two questions and answers from the Heidelberg Catechism show us the appropriate application of this teaching from God's Word. Interestingly, they are questions and answers issuing from a section having to do with the Apostles' Creed:

> Question 37: What do you understand by the word "suffered"?

> Answer: That during his whole life on earth, but especially at the end,

Christ sustained
in body and soul
the anger of God against the sin of the whole
human race.

This he did in order that,
by his suffering as the only atoning sacrifice,
he might set us free, body and soul,
from eternal condemnation,
and gain for us
God's grace,
righteousness,
and eternal life.

Question 44: Why does the Creed add: "He
descended into Hell"?

Answer: To assure me in times of personal crisis
and temptation
that Christ my Lord,
by suffering unspeakable anguish, pain, and
terror of soul,
especially on the cross but also earlier,
has delivered me from the anguish and
torment of hell.

There is nothing much to add to these most beautiful answers. Where may consolation be found in times of personal suffering? For Jonah it was in turning to God and to his temple for relief. During times of deep personal crisis and temptation for us it is in turning to the Messiah who has come. Why did Christ come into the world? "The reason the Son of God appeared was to destroy the devil's work" (1 John 3:8). Once again Christ has calmed the chaotic waters.

# FOR FURTHER REFLECTION

1. How does Jonah's descent, which begins in chapter 1, continue in chapter 2?
2. What is the meaning of life and death in the Bible? What is the significance of Sheol here?
3. What kinds of images are used in the psalm?
4. What connections can be drawn between Jonah's experience and Christ's crucifixion and resurrection?
5. Can you think of ways in which the instruction from this chapter might affect the way you respond to temptation, suffering, and affliction?

# 7

## PRAYER FROM THE DEPTHS:
## PART 2 (2:6b−9)

He is in the monstrous deep. There is nothing beneath his feet but the yielding, fleeing element. The waves, torn and scattered by the wind, close around him hideously; the rolling abyss bears him away; tatters of water are flying around his head; a populace of waves spit on him; vague openings half swallow him; each time he sinks he glimpses yawning precipices full of dark; frightful unknown tendrils seize him, bind his feet, and draw him down; he feels he is becoming the great deep; he is part of the foam; the billows toss him back and forth; he drinks in bitterness; the voracious ocean is eager to devour him; the monster plays with his agony. It is all liquid hatred to him. (Victor Hugo, *Les Misérables*)

But you brought my life up from the pit, O Lord my God. When my life was ebbing away, I remembered you, Lord, and my prayer rose to you, to your holy temple. Those who cling to worthless idols forfeit the grace that could be theirs. But I, with a song of thanksgiving,

will sacrifice to you. What I have vowed I will make
good. Salvation comes from the LORD. (Jonah 2:6b–9)


## JONAH'S WATER ORDEAL

One cannot gain even an approximate understanding
of a culture (let alone a very ancient culture) without some
kind of comprehension of its legal workings. The influence
of the legal sphere upon all aspects of culture can hardly
be overestimated. In almost every ancient civilization, and
even up into medieval law, trial by ordeal was used to determine innocence or guilt. A very common legal practice of
the cultures of the ancient Near East, judicial ordeal was
"a relatively simple procedure in which the individual at
law takes a physical test and wins or loses his legal case
on the basis of his physical response to the mechanical,
generally corporeal, trial involved."[1]

This physical ordeal could be unilateral or bilateral. For
example, in some cultures, guilt and innocence were determined by entering into bilateral combat. The ancient Near
Eastern ordeals are echoed in the Bible as well. For example, Numbers 5:11–31 prescribes an ordeal to determine the
guilt or innocence of a woman accused by her husband of
adultery (the "bitter waters" ordeal).

By far the most common kind of ordeal in Assyria was
the river or water ordeal. Kyle McCarter has succinctly summarized what this river ordeal was all about: "In the
Mesopotamian materials, a primary function of *id*, the
(divine) River, was, as is well known, to serve as a judge
in certain legal cases. Trial by river ordeal was a widespread
phenomenon, in which the accused was plunged into the
river, where his success in withstanding the rushing waters
was supposed to determine his guilt or innocence."[2]

This kind of ordeal is reflected in the famous Code of
Hammurabi, one of the most important legal texts from

ancient Mesopotamia. The second law speaks about the ordeal following an unproven accusation of sorcery:

> If a man has levied (a charge of) sorceries and then has not proved it, the one upon whom the charge of witchcraft has been laid shall go to the holy river, shall leap into the river, and if the river overwhelms him, his accuser shall carry off his house. If the river proves that man clear and he escapes safe, he who levied (the charge of) sorceries upon him shall be put to death, and he who leapt into the river shall carry off the house of his accuser.

Although this kind of practice was apparently part of the legal procedures of the day in Mesopotamia, we do not know to what extent there was any practice or even knowledge of these kinds of ordeals in ancient Israel. And yet we might say that the ideas presented above and their immediate legal practice were only "once removed" from Israel.[3] Consequently, Jonah 2 might be better understood against the conceptual backdrop of the judicial river ordeals as they were practiced in ancient Mesopotamia and other neighboring civilizations.[4]

Jonah the suppliant prophet, entombed in the belly of the large fish and knowing that his God controls the waters that overwhelm and surround him, pleads his case before the thrice-holy God who does not wink at sin. Brought low and threatened with death by drowning in the cosmic waters, Jonah cries out for mercy.

There is yet another closely related image running through this passage. It is found in the oblique references to the first exodus from the iron-furnace bondage of the Egyptians—the greatest deliverance of the Israelites. That event and the language associated with the great act of deliverance of passing through the Red Sea (which in turn is echoed in the crossing of the Jordan), and which would have far-reaching repercussions in the history of Israel and the history of the church of God, are echoed and alluded to here in the psalm of Jonah.[5] This is confirmed not just at the conceptional level (that is to say, with allusions to images) but down to the very overlap of words (e.g., *metsulah*, "the deep"; *tehom*, "the deep"; and *suf*, "seaweed") that are used in this psalm of Jonah and also are used in the Song of the Sea (Ex. 15), which is Israel's great national anthem of deliverance.

This identification of Jonah's plight as a water ordeal and the allusions to the epic motif of the exodus deliverance present the following question: Did Jesus himself conceptualize his sufferings along similar lines? After all, recent studies are confirming that the exodus event had far-reaching impact not only on the New Testament writers themselves, but even on the manner in which they organized and recorded their material. Moreover, on the mount of transfiguration, Moses and Elijah discussed with Christ his own *exodos* (exodus, departure; Luke 9:31).

Why did Christ come into the world? The apostle John answers that question for us, "The reason the Son of God appeared was to destroy the devil's work" (1 John 3:8). This answer foregrounds what is often overshadowed in our Savior's redemptive work by modern-day preachers: the active obedience of Christ.

Christ came in order to fulfill his messianic mission. This would be his own *judicial ordeal*. Just as the Lord was present with his people when they passed through the waters of the Red Sea, so also the Lord Jesus Christ would pass through the waters of John's baptism, which anticipated his battle with and ensuing triumph over the chaotic waters of death and Leviathan (in the garb of Old Testament language).[6] He defeated the draconic figure of Satan in the wilderness at the beginning of his earthly ministry, and at each ensuing turn in his earthly ministry "he learned obedience from what he suffered and, once made perfect, he became the source of eternal salvation for all who obey him" (Heb. 5:8–9). All that is to say, "Jesus saw in Jonah's trial by water the sign of his own judgment ordeal in the heart of the earth."[7]

What application and consolation for the Israel of God can be gleaned from this rich interplay of images? In the deepest anguish of God's people, he is present. When they are drowning, he is there. When God's people are afflicted, even to the point that they feel as if they are surrounded by primeval death itself, he is there. Just as God delivered them through their ordeal at the Red Sea, so he has acted again especially on Golgotha to deliver his people safely through the raging waters, defeating their foes, subduing their sin, and bringing them safe upon dry ground on the other side. The words of the prophet Isaiah comfort God's people along similar lines:

> But now, this is what the LORD says—
> > he who created you, O Jacob,
> > he who formed you, O Israel:
> "Fear not, for I have redeemed you;
> > I have summoned you by name; you are mine.
> When you pass through the waters,
> > I will be with you;
> and when you pass through the rivers,
> > they will not sweep over you;
> When you walk through the fire,
> > you will not be burned;
> > the flames will not set you ablaze.
> For I am the LORD, your God,
> > the Holy One of Israel, your Savior."
> > > (Isa. 43:1–3a)

## JONAH REDIVIVUS: JONAH'S ASCENT

Having explored the rich imagery of this psalm of Jonah as it relates to his descent into his watery grave, we now turn to explore the imagery of ascent from his watery tomb. God has been merciful to Jonah. God is a judge; even so, God is merciful to those who call upon his name. When we arrive at the end of verse 6, we have come to the psychological center of the poem.[8] Jonah's waywardness and rebellion have brought him low; God's faithfulness will raise him up.

Although Jonah declares that God has brought him up, it seems that he is about ready to lose hope. The NIV translates verse 7a, "When my life was ebbing away, I remembered you, LORD." The idiom here is the spirit or soul curling in on itself. The particular words used together to express this idea show that Jonah is about ready to lose hope.[9] Jonah is humbled. The sacrifice that God delights in most is a broken spirit. As another psalmist had stated similarly in other circumstances, "The sacrifices of God are a broken spirit; a broken and contrite heart, O God, you will not despise" (Ps. 51:17). Jonah's humility reveals a spirit cleared of self-righteous justification. The word used for his prayer (*tepillati*) not only echoes the narrator's earlier introduction (2:1) to the prayer (*wayyitpallel*), but it also embodies Jonah's appeal for mercy.

The transition from despondency and pleading for mercy toward firm resolve is captured by the next phrase, "Those who cling [*meshammerim*] to worthless idols forfeit the grace [*hesed*] that could be theirs" (v. 8). But to whom is this sunken prophet alluding while uttering this prayer? This phrase is very difficult in Hebrew. In fact, one translation (with some justification!) declares in a footnote, "meaning of Hebrew uncertain."

The NIV here translates the word *hesed* as "grace." It is a word that has received no little attention. This word is much more rich and comprehensive than the quaint English words that are often imposed upon it by translators. In fact, it is one of the words that I will leave untranslated in this book. Sasson is probably right when he says that for the present purpose it may be rendered as "the potential (as well as the fulfillment) for a person in a higher position (god, king . . .) to act favorably and benevolently to another person or entity in a lower position (nation, subject . . .)."[10] Couple this with a close study of the verb used for "forfeiting" ('*azab*), which is often used figuratively of people that forsake their God, and a picture begins to emerge that foolish idolators are in danger of losing something significant: indeed, they are about to forsake their *hesed*.

This is exactly the indictment that God takes up against his repeatedly unfaithful people throughout redemptive history. In Deuteronomy we read:

> All the nations will ask: "Why has the LORD done this to this land? Why this fierce, burning anger?"
>
> And the answer will be: "It is because this people abandoned ['*azab*] the covenant of the LORD, the God of their fathers, the covenant he made with them when he brought them out of Egypt. They went off and worshiped other gods and bowed down to them, gods they did not know, gods he had not given them." (Deut. 29:24–26)

This becomes a major and recurring theme in the prophecy of Jeremiah:

> "Be appalled at this, O heavens,
>     and shudder with great horror,"
>         declares the LORD.
> "My people have committed two sins:
> They have forsaken ['*azab*] me,
>     the spring of living water,
> and have dug their own cisterns,
>     broken cisterns that cannot hold water."
>         (Jer. 2:12–13)

Coupling such passages with Jonah 2:8 seems much less strained than seeing this verse as an allusion to the sailors in the previous chapter or an oblique reference to Jonah himself.

Rather, Jonah 2:8 seems like a reference to the Israelites, whom Jonah represents, as was discussed earlier (pp. 32–34). Recall that the constant and plaguing problem of the Israelites was covenant infidelity. The poet, therefore, has inserted this important transition at least as a caution and a warning. He seems to be saying that those who forsake their allegiance to God risk losing *hesed*. It is ambiguous whether the word as used here refers to God's *hesed* or mankind's *hesed*. I lean in the direction that the Israelites are forsaking the *hesed* (i.e., mercy) that is extended to them by their one true God since the psalmist in Psalm 144:1–2 actually calls God himself "my *hesed*":

> Praise be to the Lord my Rock,
>> who trains my hands for war,
>> my fingers for battle.
> He is my loving God [*hasdi*] and my fortress,
>> my stronghold and my deliverer,
> my shield, in whom I take refuge,
>> who subdues peoples under me.

Note that there is no equivocation here about many different ways of access to God or manifold ways of salvation: there is one God and one way of deliverance.

Another very important passage in the Bible helps clarify the point of this difficult verse: "Those who cling [*meshammerim*] to worthless idols forfeit the grace that could be theirs" (2:8). Psalm 31:6–7 is the only other place in the Hebrew Bible where the phrase "worthless idols" (*hable-shav'*) occurs:

> I hate those who cling to [*hashomerim*] worthless
> idols [*hable-shav'*];
> I trust in the LORD.
> I will be glad and rejoice in your love
> [*behasdeka*],
> for you saw my affliction
> and knew the anguish of my soul.

John Calvin shucks right to the cob, so to speak, when he poignantly says, "No aid and no help can be expected from any other quarter than from the only true God."[11]

When we come to the end of Jonah's psalm, we hear the voice of a rescued prophet snatched from the jaws of death. Jonah stared death in the face and walked away (or is it swam?) because of God's mercy. Jonah offers a *todah* to God, a token of gratitude based upon God's benevolence to him.[12] New resolve follows on the heels of deliverance. Gratitude follows mercy. Jonah now responds to his deliverance in a manner similar to how the sailors responded to their deliverance in the first chapter of the book. They feared for their lives; Jonah feared for his life. God delivered them from the fierce wrath of the storm; he delivered Jonah from the chaotic waters and the dragons of death that threatened to engulf him. A hand of mercy was extended to him.

The final line is a fitting climax to the poem: literally, "Salvation belongs to the LORD." This brief credal statement could arguably be an interpretive key to any one of the four chapters. But Jonah's language, as language always does, eventually betrays his true thinking and feelings. As we read further in the story, we will observe that Jonah is not always as enthusiastic about the application of this statement (i.e., "Salvation comes from the LORD") to others as to himself.

Many writers have compared Jonah's prayer in chapter 2 to the prayer in chapter 4, but no one has been more penetrating in his analysis of this aspect than George

Landes, who has returned to the book of Jonah time and time again throughout his scholarly career. He has noted some striking correspondences between the two chapters:[13]

| JONAH 2 | | JONAH 4 | |
|---|---|---|---|
| 1:17 | The focus shifts to Jonah | 4:1 | The focus shifts to Jonah |
| 2:10 | Jonah is spared | 4:1 | Jonah is angry because Nineveh is spared |
| 2:1 | Jonah prays | 2a | Jonah prays |
| 2–6a | He refers back to his distressing situation in the deep | 2a | He refers back to his distressing situation in Palestine |
| 6b–8 | He asserts God's merciful deliverance and draws an insight from it: idolators forsake the One who loves them | 2a | He draws an inference from the thought that God might save Nineveh: he must flee to Tarshish |
| | | 2b | He asserts the mercy of God that leads to deliverance |
| 9 | Jonah's response to Yahweh: worship with sacrifices and vows | 3 | Jonah's response to Yahweh: a plea for death |
| 10 | Yahweh's response to Jonah: he acts so that the prophet may respond favorably to the divine mission (still to be accomplished) | 4–11 | Yahweh's response to Jonah: he acts so that the prophet may respond favorably to the divine mission (already accomplished) |

Comparison of the two chapters gives evidence of Jonah's character *through time*. He has not shed all his old skin, so to speak. But that part of the story will have to remain for later.

In discussing the psalm of Jonah we have seen a remarkable Old Testament picture of death and resurrection that is mirrored in the New Testament. Jonah entered his watery grave but did not remain there. After Christ died, he was laid in his tomb, but he did not remain there. No, he was raised from the grave and appeared to many witnesses before he ascended into heaven and sat down at his heavenly Father's right hand where he now reigns in glory. But his death and resurrection were for a purpose. The apostle Paul reminds us, "He was delivered over to death for our sins and was raised to life for our justification" (Rom. 4:25).

The book of Jonah is a remarkable picture of death and deliverance from it, and this should embolden us with true assurance. We know that God will indeed make good on his promise to us when the day of eternity comes. There is no better way to close our study of the second chapter of Jonah than to turn to the words of another psalm:

> If the LORD had not been on our side—
>     let Israel say—
> if the LORD had not been on our side
>     when men attacked us,
> when their anger flared against us,
>     they would have swallowed us alive;
> the flood would have engulfed us,
>     the torrent would have swept over us,
>     the raging waters would have swept us away.
>         (Ps. 124:1–5)

## FOR FURTHER REFLECTION

1. What is a judicial trial by ordeal? What were some ways it was used in the ancient Near East?
2. How is the exodus that Israel went through related to the deliverance that Jonah experienced and to the deliverance that Christ provided?
3. How has the material in this chapter helped you understand Christ's death and resurrection in a fuller way?
4. Do you think Jonah learned humility through his near-death experience? Do you think he understood mercy?

# 8

## LESSONS ON REPENTANCE

### (2:10−3:10)

Credit praeputium et circumcisio permanet infidelis ("the foreskin believes; but circumcision remains faithless") (Jerome, *In Ionam*)

And the Lord commanded the fish, and it vomited Jonah onto dry land.

Then the word of the Lord came to Jonah a second time: "Go to the great city of Nineveh and proclaim to it the message I give you."

Jonah obeyed the word of the Lord and went to Nineveh. Now Nineveh was a very important city—a visit required three days. On the first day, Jonah started into the city. He proclaimed: "Forty more days and Nineveh will be overturned." The Ninevites believed God. They declared a fast, and all of them, from the greatest to the least, put on sackcloth.

When the news reached the king of Nineveh, he rose from his throne, took off his royal robes, covered himself with sackcloth and sat down in the dust. Then he issued a proclamation in Nineveh:

"By the decree of the king and his nobles:
    Do not let any man or beast, herd or flock,
taste anything; do not let them eat or drink. But
let man and beast be covered with sackcloth. Let
everyone call urgently on God. Let them give up
their evil ways and their violence. Who knows?
God may yet relent and with compassion turn
from his fierce anger so that we will not perish."
    When God saw what they did and how they turned
from their evil ways, he had compassion and did not
bring upon them the destruction he had threatened.
(Jonah 2:10–3:10)

In the previous chapter we witnessed God mercifully rescue Jonah from drowning. When mercy is extended to someone, the expected response is a grateful heart and changed behavior. Such was the case with Jean Valjean, one of the most famous characters in literature.

In the book *Les Misérables* by Victor Hugo, Jean Valjean is released from a long prison term for stealing a loaf of bread. He finds unexpected shelter in the home of a kind and hospitable bishop. But the old temptations prove to be too great for him. While the household is asleep, he steals some of the bishop's silver and runs off with it.

When Jean Valjean is caught red-handed with the silver in his possession, he is brought before the bishop by the authorities. At this moment we are witness to an extraordinary act of grace. The bishop informs Jean Valjean's accusers that he actually gave the silver to the ex-convict as a gift. He asks the police to remove their hands from him and allow Jean Valjean to go free immediately. Jean Valjean is mesmerized by the gesture. Hugo writes that Jean Valjean looks at the bishop with an indescribable expression. Next, the bishop takes two silver candlesticks from the mantlepiece and feigns before the police that more silver had been forgotten by his guest:

"My friend," said the bishop, "before you go away, here are your candlesticks; take them."

He went to the mantelpiece, took the two candlesticks, and handed them to Jean Valjean. . . . Jean Valjean was trembling all over. He took the two candlesticks distractedly, with a bewildered expression.

"Now," said the bishop, "go in peace. By the way, my friend, when you come again, you needn't come through the garden. You can always come and go by the front door. It is only closed with a latch, day or night."

Next, after the gendarmes had left, the bishop admonishes Jean Valjean:

"Do not forget, ever, that you promised me to use this silver to become an honest man." Jean Valjean, who had no recollection of any such promise, stood dumbfounded. The bishop had stressed these words as he spoke them. He continued solemnly, "Jean Valjean, my brother, you no longer belong to evil; but to good. It is your soul I am buying for you. I withdraw it from dark thoughts and from the spirit of perdition, and I give it to God!"

This merciful act made such an impression upon the troubled convict that it left him indelibly changed forever. Having been the recipient of unspeakable mercies, he now becomes the benefactor of one merciful act after another toward the outcast and suffering: he rescues a destitute and disadvantaged woman turned prostitute; he saves a man about to be crushed under a cart and later finds employment for him; he protects the woman's daughter from a situation of child-slavery and treats her as his own granddaughter. Mercy had worked a powerful transformation in his life and character.

One would think that the mercy extended to Jonah in the intestines of the Leviathan would have had similar effects; nevertheless, as we move into the second half of the book of Jonah, we will observe that it was not so. Or, the effects were only short-lived.

## JONAH'S REPENTANCE

As one author has said, "In chapter 3 the plot rewinds and begins again."[1] This is indicated in a couple of ways. First, in 2:10, there is a break in the text indicated by the Hebrew consonant *peh*. This instructed the ancient scribes to leave a space in the text vacant since there was a natural break.

Second, a comparison of the similarities and differences in the way chapters 1 and 3 begin is striking:

| CHAPTER 1 | CHAPTER 3 |
|---|---|
| 1. *The word of the LORD came to Jonah* son of Amittai: | 1. *Then the word of the LORD came to Jonah* a second time: |
| 2. *"Go to the great city of Nineveh and* preach against it, because its wickedness has come up before me." | 2. *"Go to the great city of Nineveh and* proclaim to it the message I give you." |
| 3. But Jonah ran away from the LORD and headed for Tarshish. He went down to Joppa, where he found a ship bound for that port. After paying the fare, he went aboard and sailed for Tarshish to flee from the LORD. | 3. Jonah obeyed the word of the LORD and went to Nineveh. Now Nineveh was a very important city—a visit required three days |

There are many intriguing differences and similarities between these verses, but three in particular stand out: in verse 1, "a second time" has replaced the patronymic name;

God now has a very specific message for Jonah to deliver; and unlike the first encounter, Jonah obeys God's command this time.

What is in sharpest contrast is the difference in the content of 1:3 and 3:3. In a previous chapter we discussed Jonah's rebellion in detail. We observed that at the very beginning of the book, Jonah's disobedience is described in stark contrast to God's stated will. Jonah's disobedience is emphasized by the words in 1:3, "But Jonah ran away." The fact that the author takes pains to emphasize that he fled is evident from the fact that "*from the* LORD" occurs two times in this verse.

In chapter 3 of the story, however, we may think that Jonah has learned the lessons God was seeking to teach him. But when we come to chapter 4, we will begin to understand that Jonah, just like ourselves, has many more depths to plumb before he begins to grasp the knowledge of God and his ways in the world. Nevertheless, Jonah takes his message to Nineveh, and surprisingly, Nineveh repents.

We have already discussed what the mention of the name of Nineveh probably meant for the ancient Hebrew. At this point in the story there is an interruption half-way through verse 3 with some new circumstantial material: "Now Nineveh was a very important city—a visit required three days."

The Hebrew language in verse 3 is much more specific than the NIV indicates. It reads literally, "Now Nineveh was a large city to the gods" or "a large city to/for God." Nineveh is called "a large city" in four places in the book of Jonah (see 1:2; 3:2, 3; and 4:11). The first of the proposed translations, which would emphasize the importance of Nineveh to the many gods of the Assyrians, is probably not the correct one. Although the Bible is often polemical in its language toward the idols and gods of Israel's neighbors, that doesn't seem to fit the story logic at this point. If the latter translation, which is also a literal translation, is adopted, then the grammatical construction would seem to emphasize that this city—albeit a pagan one—belongs to the one true God of the universe. The city is God's. The fact that God, the God of Israel, owns foreign cities and nations as well as Israel is a well-worn lesson perhaps; nevertheless, it seems to be a lesson that needs repeating.

This interpretation fits well with the credal statement we already observed on the lips of Jonah as he was caught in the storm with the sailors: "I am a Hebrew and I worship the LORD, the God of heaven, who made the sea and the land" (1:9). That statement implies that the Lord owns all created things and therefore the city of Nineveh as well. Thus, through this added detail, the Israelites were reminded of "God's dominion over the staunchest of Israel's foes."[2]

One more detail of the text needs discussion before we move on. The NIV translates the last phrase of 1:3 to suggest that Nineveh is large enough to require a three-day visit. There is no merit whatsoever to the translation which literally reads "a three days' journey," a phrase that has been shown to be figurative in use.[3] The phrase is actually intended to indicate that the city is very far away when Jonah begins his journey of six hundred miles—much more than a literal three days' journey. The phrase is not meant, therefore, to describe the size of the city or the length of Jonah's stay; rather, it is used figuratively and idiomatically to express the long distance Jonah would have to travel in order to arrive at Nineveh.[4] Whenever a short distance was intended, the ancients would say "a one day's journey." This is the phrase that begins the next verse (v. 4); it explains that Jonah had not gone very far into the city before he began his preaching.

So what does Jonah do once he arrives at the Big Apple of ancient Assyria? He begins proclaiming the message: a brief pronouncement of imminent destruction (only five words in Hebrew!). One commentator has said, "Its five

Hebrew words . . . constitute the briefest prophetic denunciation on record."[5] The Ninevites seem to have clearly interpreted his words to be a pronouncement about possible imminent destruction since the edict of the king in verse 9 says: "Who knows? God may yet relent and with compassion turn from his fierce anger so that we will not perish." They interpreted Jonah's prophecy as one of doom, pure and simple.

The word used when Jonah describes the portending overthrow (hapak; here a niphal participle, nehpaket) can have either the meaning "be overturned" or "be turned, transformed" (i.e., to God). Since it can also have this meaning of "transform," many commentators play with the idea that a double entendre (two meanings) is communicated through this ambiguity. In fact, commentators are almost evenly divided over the issue of whether the author meant to communicate one or both meanings simultaneously. Nevertheless, it seems that the context rules out the meaning of transformation at least with respect to how the Ninevites themselves interpreted the word used (hapak). Moreover, the very language used by Jonah undoubtedly had strong evocations of the episode with Sodom and Gomorrah overturned (hapak) by God's judgment, a leitmotif throughout the Old Testament (Gen. 19:25, 29; Deut. 29:23; Isa. 13:19; Jer. 20:16; 49:18; 50:40; Lam. 4:6; Amos 4:11). Those passages employ language similar to what is seen here in Jonah. Apparently Jonah's words put the fear of God in the Ninevites.

So Jonah was made compliant. Unlike his behavior in chapter 1, where he strives to flee from God and his commission, he fulfills his mission in chapter 3.

## NINEVEH'S REPENTANCE

Seeing the paintings of Vincent Van Gogh was one of the highlights of my life when we lived on the East Coast (they were on loan from the Netherlands to the National Gallery). One of my favorite Van Gogh paintings (which was unfortunately not on display) comes from the St. Rémy-Anvers period at the end of Van Gogh's life. It was in the asylum at St. Rémy that Van Gogh allegedly experienced nostalgia for his religious past. His pilgrimage through life came to its end there, an end that unfortunately he himself precipitated when he took his own life.[6]

The painting I have in mind is entitled "At Eternity's Gate." The subject is an old man seated in a chair, with his head in his hand. Van Gogh probably identified himself with this chair and this man. (In earlier paintings such as "The Potato Eaters," the chair appears with Van Gogh's signature etched upon it.) We see that the old man is to be most pitied. Hope for happiness in this lifetime is lost upon the old man who is "At Eternity's Gate." The painting manifests profound sorrow. Indeed, for me Van Gogh's artistry captures the predicament of modern man—and ancients also—and their great need for true repentance.

What was the response of the Ninevites to Jonah's preaching? Belief and acceptance; in a word, it was total repentance. The repentance of Nineveh in Jonah acts as a foil ("foil" is a literary term to describe either a character or an event that is used to contrast another character or element in the story). In our story, Nineveh behaves as a foil for our main character Jonah. Indeed, "the Assyrian capital is used as a foil to win the final salvation of Jonah, if like the Ninevites he will but repent and change his thinking about the objective of divine mercy."[7] The strange fact that we are now presented with the "peculiarity of a narrative about a snow-white Assyria"[8] serves as a marvelous contrast for the lack of repentance that eventually becomes evident in the prophet's life.

Moreover, since Jonah represents Israel, the author has used Nineveh as a foil to indict Israel indirectly for her own lack of repentance. The fact that the story makes use of the capital city of the Assyrians, renowned for their infamous and violent treatment of their neighbors, serves as a fitting—albeit indirect—condemnation of the chosen nation that had grown complacent in its own zeal for righteousness and holiness. This is different from the all-too-common assumption among commentators that the purpose of this little prophecy is to rebuke Israel for her xenophobic hatred of non-Israelites (supposedly deriving from the theology contemporaneous with the late date of the book's composition). That is not what I'm asserting; rather, I am asserting something quite different; namely, that what is being rebuked is lack of compliance on Israel's part to the prophetic preaching of God's Word. This is in stark contrast to the behavior observed in the Ninevites, Israel's enemy.

Israel alone among all the nations of the earth was to be the apple of God's eye. And Israel's obedience to God was to be a source of blessing to the other nations observing her. Consider what Scripture says about God's view of Israel's role among the nations:

> Observe them [the commandments] carefully, for this will show your wisdom and understanding to the nations, who will hear about all these decrees and say, "Surely this great nation is a wise and understanding people." What other nation is so great as to have their gods near them the way the LORD our God is near us whenever we pray to him? And what other nation is so great as to have such righteous decrees and laws as this body of laws I am setting before you today? (Deut. 4:6–8)

Or again in the book of 1 Kings:

> May the LORD our God be with us as he was with our fathers; may he never leave us nor forsake us. May

he turn our hearts to him, to walk in all his ways and to keep the commands, decrees and regulations he gave our fathers. And may these words of mine, which I have prayed before the LORD, be near to the LORD our God day and night, that he may uphold the cause of his servant and the cause of his people Israel according to each day's need, so that all the peoples of the earth may know that the LORD is God and that there is no other. But your hearts must be fully committed to the LORD our God, to live by his decrees and obey his commands, as at this time. (1 Kings 8:57–61)

Tragically, the historical sections of God's Word provide abundant evidence of Israel's continued and recalcitrant unfaithfulness to the stipulations set out by her covenant Lord. If the people refuse to obey, if they refuse to magnify God's name among the surrounding nations, then God will purify his unrepentant people through exile, but also through restoration from exile so that the nations may see the power of God's name again. Israel's obedience was intended to signify God's glory among the nations. If she failed in that obedience, then she would be chastised and disciplined. And God would still have glory.

When we arrive at 3:5, we see the sudden flowering up of this important theme of repentance. The text first gives a general overview and then the bottom line of the effect upon the populace: "The Ninevites believed God. They declared a fast, and all of them, from the greatest to the least, put on sackcloth."

The text is out of chronological order here. Such artistic grouping of events should not trouble the reader of the Bible, for it is not an uncommon technique (see, e.g., Ps. 114). Such deformation in chronological sequencing for literary or theological purposes is not a sign of sloppy editorial work, as many in the past often thought; rather, it can be a sign of artistic genius.[9] The king's decree (vv. 7–9) actually comes before the people's fast and repentance, but the narrator wants to give the bottom line—a general overview—before he backs up in order to fill in the details of how this widespread repentance came to be. The king first issues a decree and sets the example, and the people follow. This line of interpretation stretches back at least to Rabbi Ibn Ezra, a great Jewish Bible scholar from Spain (ca. 1089–1164).

The Hebrew word for "repentance" (*shub*) occurs four times in Jonah. Significantly, all four occurrences are in the space of these few verses (vv. 8–10), signaling the emergence of a new and important theme. In fact, some think that the author's primary preoccupation is to focus the reader's attention on this very theme of repentance and the consequences of whether one has repentance or not.[10]

## GOD'S REPENTANCE

Our text in Jonah 3:10 introduces us to some difficult theological issues that have been the topic of recent debates. In order to understand God's relationship to his creatures, we need to discuss briefly a subject that, though heady, is nevertheless extremely important. I have in mind the topic of open theism. The subject into which we are about to dive has a serious effect upon the comfort and consolation of people who are suffering. Consequently, we need to digress slightly in order to understand the conclusion of chapter 3.

Verse 10 of Jonah 3 raises questions of God's immutability and, ultimately, his sovereignty. Does God know everything that will take place in the world? Furthermore, does he actually determine or decree everything that will take place in the future as certain passages in the Bible would seem to suggest (see, e.g., Ps. 33:11 and Eph. 1:11)? It has been customarily taught that such an understanding of God's providence has the net effect of producing joy, comfort, and assurance in the life and soul of the child of God. In fact, meditating on God's goodness and providential care during times of severe suffering or affliction has been a way to overcome bitterness.

Consider, for example, the psalms which emphasize God's care for his own, particularly Psalm 55:22, "Cast your cares on the LORD and he will sustain you; he will never let the righteous fall." Or again, Psalm 91:1, "He who dwells in the shelter of the Most High will rest in the shadow of the Almighty." Such passages should help the child of God develop a quiet and composed mind in the midst of perplexing circumstances (see Isa. 49:15, 25; Zech. 2:8; 1 Peter 5:6–7). After all, if God does not allow a hair from his child to be harmed without his knowing and willing it, doesn't that bring great assurance to the child of God as he or she passes through this sin-cursed world (Matt. 10:28–31)? Indeed, this view of God's providence has always been a source of great comfort to his people: when vexed by the sufferings and afflictions so common to human existence, one can truly know that God is just and good in all his administrations in the world. Even when another human being becomes the agent delivering the blow of suffering or injustice, then a child of God may console herself with the truth that a sovereign and just Lord in heaven has allowed it to happen.

But is another interpretation of events possible? Is God's decree changeable on the basis of the actions of creatures here on earth? Some passages in the Bible would seem possibly to suggest this at first glance (e.g., Gen. 6:7; 1 Sam. 15:35; Ps. 106:45). Is the future undetermined by God? More immediately germane to our text, what exactly does it mean when God relents (or "repents" in some translations) of punishment that he threatened to carry out against recalcitrant sinners who suddenly change their ways? Does this mean that God's decree does not stand firm and is actually open to alteration based upon the conduct of creatures here below? Such would seem to be the case from such a passage as Jeremiah 18:7–10, where we read:

> If at any time I announce that a nation or kingdom is to be uprooted, torn down and destroyed, and if that nation I warned repents of its evil, then I will relent and not inflict on it the disaster I had planned. And if at another time I announce that a nation or kingdom is to be built up and planted, and if it does evil in my sight and does not obey me, then I will reconsider the good I had intended to do for it.

These questions confront us here at the end of the third chapter of Jonah. Older translations of Jonah 3:10 (e.g., KJV and RSV) translate this verse in a way that may be unclear for the modern reader: "And God saw their works, that they turned from their evil way; and God repented of the evil, that he had said that he would do unto them; and he did it not" (KJV). Such a translation of the Hebrew verb (*naham*) may not have caused as much trouble for the English reader four hundred years ago, but it is problematic for the modern reader, especially in the light of recent developments in evangelical theology.

"To repent" for the modern reader means to repent or turn from some wrongdoing. Obviously that is not the case with God. However, even when the idea of "repenting" connotes only the idea of change of mind, that is, relenting, even so there is need of further explanation lest people derive the wrong notion concerning God's decree and constancy relative to the actions of creatures. Furthermore, the potential for further confusion is exacerbated for many Christians today because of the new movement in evangelical theology called open theism.

Scholars such as John Sanders, Clark Pinnock, and Gregory Boyd are representative of this new movement. The issue that the open theists wish to raise is not a new one; it has actually been a point of discussion throughout various periods in the history of the church.[11] Is the classic orthodox understanding of God's *immutability* (constancy, unchangeableness, evidenced by such texts as Mal. 3:6; James 1:17) correct, or does it need to be revised in light of such scriptural passages as those quoted above?

Gregory Boyd's book *God of the Possible* is a good place to start in trying to understand this theological movement because he writes with a general audience in mind. For Boyd, the issue is not about God's omniscience, that is to say, his knowing everything. Rather, the issue is "about the nature of the reality that God perfectly knows."[12]

The classic view, as Boyd recounts accurately, is that everything in the future is settled and fixed, eternally foreknown and predestined by a sovereign God. It is important at this point in the discussion to note also that the orthodox position has always taken pains to assert that God is not the author of evil. Crimes are not turned into virtues, as Calvin reminded us, simply because someone is carrying out the preordained plan of God. No. In the classic Reformed position, evil is squarely laid at the feet of the evildoer, not God.

For Boyd, however, this classic view found its way into the church because of the influence of Greek philosophical notions that supposedly poisoned the thinking of those who were originally clarifying the doctrine of God's immutability or unchangeableness and its relation to God's decree. By contrast, open theists

hold that the future consists partly of settled realities and partly of unsettled realities. Some things about the future are *possibly* this way and *possibly* that way. Hence, precisely because they also hold that God knows all of reality perfectly, open theists believe that God knows the future as consisting of both unsettled possibilities and settled certainties. In this sense, open theists could (and should) affirm that God knows the future perfectly. It's just that they understand the future *as it is now* to include genuine possibilities.[13]

This is categorically different from the classical position; Boyd calls attention to a group of passages from Scripture that introduce the "motif of future openness," passages that depict "God as facing a partly open future. He does not control and/or foreknow exactly what is going to happen."[14]

Now when a person reading the Scriptures runs up against a passage such as Jonah 3:10 and reads that passage with the notion of undetermined future events in mind—the view that "in Scripture we find that God changes his mind in response to events that transpire in history"[15]—one may begin to understand how such passages might foreground hard questions for the reader who holds the classic view. Boyd, for example, in treating Jonah 3:10 among a group of related passages says, "God '*changed his mind*' about the destruction he planned to carry out on Nineveh. Note, neither this nor any other verse says or even remotely suggests that God *appeared* to change his mind. It simply says, in as plain and straightforward a way as can be imagined, that God 'changed his mind.' "[16]

Indeed, the questions raised by open theists such as Boyd and others are important and should be taken seriously. Nevertheless, the conclusions arrived at are questionable on a number of grounds and may possibly erode a person's assurance and consolation during times of deep distress and suffering.

Views such as open theism are not altogether new and have received intelligent, sustained, and engaged rebuttals in the past.[17] Exploring that trail here would take us too far astray from our main task, so we cannot deal with the views represented in *God of the Possible* in great detail. However, a few words are necessary to explain how a modern reader may read difficult passages such as Jonah 3:10 and not compromise the Scripture's teaching of God's decrees and immutability.

Returning to our passage in Jonah, I contend that the bottom line for Boyd's position on Jonah and other passages touching on what he calls the "motif of future openness" is faulty because he does not understand the nature of how language works in Scripture. Other aspects could be discussed, but this is one of the major weaknesses of the views of open theists. Before we discuss the matter any further, therefore, it is necessary to briefly discuss the nature of scriptural language.

We must not forget before whom we stand. God is infinite in majesty. His ways are not totally comprehensible to creatures. Therefore, Scripture speaks to us in terms of *analogical* discourse. This is not a new or recent way of talking about the nature of scriptural language. One Reformed apologist, Michael Horton, has said: "When one says that 'God is good' and 'Sally is good,' the predicate 'good' is used neither univocally (i.e., identically) nor equivocally (i.e., with no actual similarity), but analogically. Analogical thinking, then, identifies certain aspects of the unknown in terms of the known and familiar."[18]

Cornelius Van Til, the apologist at Westminster Seminary who labored alongside J. Gresham Machen, expressed himself in similar terms when he talked about the system of Scripture being an analogical system.[19] None of what has just now been asserted calls into question the veracity or truthfulness of Scripture. Quite the contrary.

These apologists stand in a long tradition of theology that has recognized and grappled with the nature of scriptural revelation. For example, Calvin argued strenuously that God's truth is accommodated to our capacity as finite creatures. In Calvin's terms, God talks to us in baby talk. As a mother stoops to talk to a child, so God speaks to us in such terms that we may grasp his truth. These kinds of categories enabled those wrestling with the meaning of difficult passages of Scripture to handle sensitively figures of speech, metaphors, and the question of when a passage should be taken literally and when figuratively.

For example, when the Bible speaks to us about God and his relations with his creatures, it often speaks in language that is *anthropomorphic* (i.e., it ascribes human characteristics to a being that is not human, i.e., to God). Sometimes Scripture uses *anthropopathisms* (it ascribes human emotions or passions to God) as well when speaking about God's relations and actions with human beings. Being aware of these matters helps students of the Bible, professionals and laypersons alike, to interpret the authors of Scripture as they intended their writings to be understood.

An example is the description of God's grieving at the way mankind had become so morally destitute just before the flood: "The LORD saw how great man's wickedness on the earth had become, and that every inclination of the thoughts of his heart was only evil all the time. The LORD was grieved that he had made man on the earth, and his heart was filled with pain" (Gen. 6:5–6). The passage says that God "saw," and yet God does not have eyes like men. The passage also says that he was "grieved," but this is different from a man's or woman's regret or grief. The language is meant to communicate similarity to human grief but also something quite different when applied to the almighty Creator, Redeemer, and Sustainer of the universe.

The distinctions and differences between the Creator and the creature should always be borne in mind, especially when it comes to feelings described. It is not that God does not have emotions or feelings toward his creatures, but he is not, for example, moved to anger as we human beings are; he does not "fly off the handle," so to speak.

What God does when he speaks to us in his Word is accommodate to our weakness. Along these lines John Calvin has expressed in very helpful terms how we may understand God's workings and providence in light of those passages that talk of God's "repentance":

> What, therefore, does the word "repentance" mean? Surely its meaning is like that of all other modes of speaking that describe God for us in human terms. For because our weakness does not attain to his exalted state, the description of him that is given to us must be accommodated to our capacity so that we may understand it. Now the mode of accommodation is for him to represent himself to us not as he is in himself, but as he seems to us. Although he is beyond all disturbance of mind, yet he testifies that he is angry toward sinners. Therefore whenever we hear that God is angered, we ought not to imagine any emotion in him, but rather to consider that this expression has been taken from our own human experience. . . . So we ought not to understand anything else under the word "repentance" than change of action, because men are wont by changing their action to testify that they are displeased with themselves. Therefore, since every change among men is a correction of what displeases them, but that correction arises out of repentance, then by the word "repentance" is meant the fact that God changes with respect to his actions. Meanwhile neither God's plan nor his will is reversed, nor his volition altered; but what he had from eternity foreseen, approved, and decreed he pursues in uninterrupted tenor, however sudden the variation may appear in men's eyes.[20]

An appreciation for the complex nature of how language works in Scripture will, then, aid us in understanding difficult passages such as Jonah 3:10. Perhaps more importantly, such an appreciation of how scriptural language works will also aid us in wrestling with the problems of suffering, affliction, and injustices not only in our own lives but in the lives of others as well. God is not capricious. If we are honest men and women, there will indeed be times when we will struggle greatly under the weight of a so-called frowning providence. Nevertheless, we may always reassure ourselves with confidence that God is on his throne and that his house (i.e., his world) is in order. God is never taken by surprise, nor is he ever mesmerized or baffled by any turn of events.

Ultimately and some day, all injustices will be eternally adjudicated. Even when bad things happen to "good" people, it is not outside the purview of our heavenly Father, "the compassionate and gracious God, slow to anger, abounding in love [*hesed*] and faithfulness, maintaining love to thousands, and forgiving wickedness, rebellion and sin. Yet he does not leave the guilty unpunished" (Ex. 34:6–7).

## FOR FURTHER REFLECTION

1. In keeping with the theme in Jonah's prayer that, "Salvation comes from the LORD," deliverance obviously came to Jonah in chapter 2. To whom does it come in chapter 3 and why?
2. Compare the opening verses of chapter 1 with the opening verses of chapter 3. What does this tell you about the development of the plot and Jonah's character?
3. Jonah's message is reminiscent of the narrative of Sodom and Gomorrah being destroyed (Gen. 19).

Reread Genesis 18–19 and compare Abraham's role and intercession in that narrative with Jonah's role in Jonah 3–4. Did Christ ever lament over or intercede on behalf of a city; if so, how did our Lord's actions compare with those of Jonah and Abraham?

4. What would the notion of the repentance of the Ninevites have communicated to the original Jewish audience?

5. Summarize the recent debates about God's "repentance."

6. Why is this current theological discussion important, and what questions does it raise about the nature of God?

# 9

# THE FINAL DEBATE (4:1–11)

Yea, woe to him who, as the great Pilot Paul has it, while preaching to others is himself a castaway! (Herman Melville, *Moby Dick*)

Hence no one will be a willing Prophet or Teacher, except he is persuaded that God is merciful. (John Calvin, *Commentary on Jonah*)

But Jonah was greatly displeased and became angry. He prayed to the LORD, "O LORD, is this not what I said when I was still at home? That is why I was so quick to flee to Tarshish. I knew that you are a gracious and compassionate God, slow to anger and abounding in love, a God who relents from sending calamity. Now, O LORD, take away my life, for it is better for me to die than to live."

But the LORD replied, "Have you any right to be angry?"

Jonah went out and sat down at a place east of the city. There he made himself a shelter, sat in its shade and waited to see what would happen to the city. Then the LORD God provided a vine and made it grow up over

Jonah to give shade for his head to ease his discomfort, and Jonah was very happy about the vine. But at dawn the next day God provided a worm, which chewed the vine so that it withered. When the sun rose, God provided a scorching east wind, and the sun blazed on Jonah's head so that he grew faint. He wanted to die, and said, "It would be better for me to die than to live."

But God said to Jonah, "Do you have a right to be angry about the vine?"

"I do," he said, "I am angry enough to die."

But the LORD said, "You have been concerned about this vine, though you did not tend it or make it grow. It sprang up overnight and died overnight. But Nineveh has more than a hundred and twenty thousand people who cannot tell their right hand from their left, and many cattle as well. Should I not be concerned about that great city?" (Jonah 4:1–11)

"Anger is one letter away from danger!" So reads the little marquee at a gas station just down the road. How true it is. In the preceding chapter the focus was on repentance. In Jonah 4 our wayward prophet is in danger of allowing his anger to be focused not only on Nineveh, but on God as well; for the emphasis of chapter 4 is on Jonah's reaction to the display of God's mercy.

Chapter 4 begins by saying, "But Jonah was greatly displeased and became angry." This verse is directly connected with the last verse in chapter 3. The term "was displeased" translates a Hebrew word that has been used repeatedly throughout the book in different ways (*vayyera‘* from the root *r‘*). Usually when this Hebrew verb is used, it occurs in conjunction with the eyes (e.g., "it was evil in the eyes of . . ."). This common Hebrew idiom is another way of saying that someone thinks something is wrong.[1]

The actual subject (an impersonal one) of this verb (*vayyera‘*) is "it" and not Jonah as the NIV translates the sentence.[2] Therefore, the verse should be translated, "It displeased Jonah greatly." Consequently, we are led to ask, to what does the "it" refer? That question is answered by turning back to the previous chapter: the "it" refers to two things which displease Jonah: the Ninevites turning from their violent and wicked ways and God "repenting" of the action he had stated he was going to perform.

This does not displease Jonah a little. It displeases him greatly! We earlier noted (p. 51) a feature of Hebrew that makes an expression more emphatic. When a Hebrew writer wished to strengthen the verbal force, he used as the object of the verb a noun built from the same consonants as the verb (*vayyera'* . . . *ra'ah gedolah*). Literally, verse 1 reads, "It was evil to Jonah a great evil, and it burned to him."

Jonah is a roller coaster of emotions; in this chapter he displays anger, which is the complete opposite of the thankful and praise-filled spirit of chapter 2. Jack Sasson summarizes this well: "Although some prophets will sometimes feel abandoned by God or will occasionally denounce the grinding demands God makes on them, none but Jonah experiences as many emotional fluctuations within so brief a narrative."[3] So before we examine God's response, we need to explore the contours of Jonah's sullen attitude.

## JONAH'S FRUSTRATION

In the initial verses of chapter 4, irony seems to jump off the page. For example, did you notice the strange fact that a prophet of God is actually *displeased* when a city of sinners experiences a tremendous moral reform and responds to the Word of God? Indeed, upon Nineveh's repentant response to the prophet's message, Jonah becomes despondent and angry and even expresses a death wish (v. 3), "passive suicide."[4]

In verse 2, Jonah enters into prayer again. But this is not the prayer of chapter 2; in chapter 4 we are given an insight into why he fled in the first place—knowing that God is merciful, Jonah utters a complaint. We earlier observed the striking similarities and differences between the prayer in chapter 2 and the prayer here in chapter 4. In short, when he prayed in chapter 2, "it was an expression of submission to God's greater might; when spoken from outside the city of Nineveh [chapter 4], it is a protest against God's compassionate nature."[5]

The divine attributes that Jonah cites are taken from a well-known list in Exodus 34:6–7 (also Neh. 9:17; Pss. 86:15; 103:8; 145:8; Joel 2:13–14). Jonah does not wish God to be true to himself. Or, at least, he wishes that God be not so generous in his merciful attributes but a little more liberal in the attributes of justice—something noticeably missing from Jonah's list but not from Exodus 34:6–7 and Numbers 14:18.[6] Sullenly, Jonah quotes God's word back to him, and it becomes evident how blind Jonah's despondency has made him.

Jonah is not yet reconciled to the desire and will of God. Jonah is frustrated. Nineveh is not going to be punished. God is going to be true to his revelation: he is kind and compassionate, slow to anger and abounding in *hesed*.

One of Jonah's quintessential problems is that he has forgotten God's mercy toward him. Jonah is suffering from a memory problem. He too has experienced God's mercy, but now he is ill-equipped to appreciate God's mercy when he observes it exercised on someone else's behalf. The story is again thick with irony because "Jonah now desires to die on account of God's gracious and compassionate nature. Had he himself not benefited from these very attributes when confronted with death (2:7–8)?"[7]

So what is God's method with Jonah? God is about to engage Jonah in a counseling session that Jonah will never forget. He both poses searching questions and uses a parable from nature to help the prophet "get it." In other words, he depersonalizes the situation by the use of a little parable so that Jonah may engage God's instruction from another angle. He enters into a bit of experiential education with Jonah. Jonah wanted justice; God gave mercy. One author nailed it when he summarized: "But the Lord utterly repudiates his [Jonah's] basic premise that mercy must not be intermingled with justice. It is an error that cannot be eradicated from his heart by additional information, but only by personal experience that will open his eyes to a clearer perception of himself, other human beings, and his God."[8]

God begins to teach Jonah by asking him questions. Question asking is often the manner of divine pedagogy. Think of the garden of Eden and the questions put to Adam and Eve: "Where are you? . . . Who told you that you were naked? Have you eaten from the tree that I commanded you not to eat from? . . . What is this you have done?" (Gen. 3:9–13). In the book of Job, God checks his servant's attitude by means of questions: "Who is this that darkens my counsel with words without knowledge? Brace yourself like a man; I will question you, and you shall answer me" (Job 38:2–3). Similarly, God poses three questions to Jonah. Those questions are one key to understanding the climax of the book. The author of Jonah has been holding us in suspense until this point.

God begins questioning Jonah in verse 4, "Have you any right to be angry?" In Hebrew the question is just three short words. The way the question is phrased (with *lak* in Hebrew toward the end) makes it clear that God wants Jonah to look inward. "He [God] reminds Jonah to examine his own heart, as though he said, 'Look on thyself as in a mirror: thou wilt see what a boisterous sea is thy soul, being seized as thou art by so mad a rage.' "[9]

The implication might very well be to question whether Jonah is right in passing judgment upon God's decision to grant mercy at this point. Jonah turns his anger upon himself and becomes full of "sulky despair."[10] Perhaps the Hebrew writer is describing a depression from anger turned reflexively against oneself.[11]

But God's question in verse 4 probes deeper still to show the real profundity of Jonah's problem. It shows the root of Jonah's sin. In verse 5 Jonah goes outside, east of Nineveh, and sits down. This is a place for him to watch (to see if the Ninevites would persevere in repentance?), to pray, to experience a different kind of storm than in chapter 1, and to receive a theophany, that is, a manifestation or appearance of God.

Jonah builds for himself a shelter (*sukkah*). This is a booth. The word is related to the plural word for "the feast of tabernacles" (*sukkot*). Such a shelter or booth (often translated "tabernacle") "symbolizes God's wondrous providence and covenant with Israel."[12] How ironic!

The prophet sits in his private retreat, a little resort where he can wait upon the hill and watch for what will happen to the city. One can understand Jonah's desire for shelter given the relatively bleak setting of the environs of Nineveh. Like many ancient Near Eastern cities, the landscape would have been hot and arid. Jonah shows himself to be a man still in human skin, prone to wander and sin, inclined to give in to anger, despair, and self-justification in spite of his transformation in the fish.[13]

In verse 6, God graciously appoints a vine to grow up in the night alongside Jonah's booth to shade (*tsel*) him and to save him (*lehatsil lo*)—another pun. And from what does this vine save him? It saves him from his discomfort (*ra'ato*). The author has provided a nice echo of verse 1, calling attention back to Jonah's great displeasure (ra'ah gedolah). Just as God provided the fish, now he also appoints the plant. We observe another irony when Jonah rejoices with great joy over his own deliverance (4:1, 6), yet he expresses grief over the deliverance of the Ninevites.

Bible scholars debate over what the plant could have been (e.g., a "ricinus plant" or a "castor-oil" plant), but a firm identification doesn't help to explain the nature parable that God is about ready to use. In verse 7, at dawn God appoints a worm to gnaw away at Jonah's shade-giving plant (a qiqayon). The Hebrew word for "dawn" probably provides further echoes with other words used in chapter 4. As we have clearly seen, the writer of Jonah enjoyed the literary technique of pun-making, and especially in this chapter.

The Lord now follows these events by turning up the heat, so to speak. God sends a sirocco, a hot east wind (see Ex. 14:21).[14] This is a natural phenomenon that may not immediately resonate with those of us who don't work outdoors regularly or live in the Near East. Those of us who sit in front of a computer screen or work indoors most of the day may not always be sensitized to the use of natural phenomena for images and metaphors in the Bible.

The sirocco, the hot east wind coming down from the mountains of Iran, was especially well known in the land of Israel (Arabic, khamsin). This wind can often be extremely oppressive, reaching speeds of sixty miles per hour. For those who live in Los Angeles or San Diego, the same meteorological conditions are almost exactly represented in the Santa Ana winds that have contributed to the worst fires in the history of California. Such imagery derived from natural phenomena is regularly used for theological purposes in the Bible of the ancient Jewish people, sometimes even to represent a manifestation of God to man (see Nah. 2:1–8). So now the rays of the sun beat down upon shadeless Jonah, and God also sends a sirocco. Again Jonah wishes death over life.

The second question from God occurs in verse 9. This verse, like verse 4, has to do with the rightness of Jonah's anger. Before it was anger over the deliverance of the city of Nineveh; now Jonah's anger is vented toward the destruction of a plant.

In these closing climactic verses, God uses a kind of argument known as "from the lesser to the greater" or *qal vahomer*. Literally "light and heavy," the Hebrew phrase was extremely common in rabbinic literature as a rule for interpretation of Scripture. It sets up a parallelism, or more precisely an antiparallelism, between things being compared. However, the balance between the parts is sometimes less than perfect, as it is here. Indeed, forcing exact and rigorous symmetry between the parts being compared can lead to a faulty interpretation.

The rabbis loved to use this method of argumentation. It is used to introduce the second term of an *a fortiori* comparison (if . . . *how much more!*). Even a cursory reading of the Sermon on the Mount (Matt. 5–7) will demonstrate that it was one of our Lord's favorite methods for teaching. For example, "If you, then, though you are evil, know how to give good gifts to your children, how much more will your Father in heaven give good gifts to those who ask him!" (Matt. 7:11). Additionally, the apostle Paul was inclined to use *qal vahomer* arguments frequently.

Jonah brought the almighty God before the bar of justice and proclaimed him guilty. Now God has had enough. John Calvin gives an apt summary of Jonah's behavior when he says, "And it is certainly a most unseemly thing, when a mean creature rises up against God, and in a boisterous spirit contends with him: this is monstrous; and Jonah was in this state of mind."[15] God is going to debate with Jonah using *qal vahomer* argumentation.

How did the plant come to Jonah? As a gift or something that he deserved of his own merit? As a gift of course. He did not work for it or tend it, and yet he is tremendously grieved about losing it. Look at verse 10 and see how this is made even more explicit. The plant came in one day! You, Jonah, did not create, take care of, or nurture the plant. I, however, did all this for Nineveh. The plant appeared overnight, but Nineveh grew up over many months and years and has very many people in it. How much more does it deserve care, concern, pity! Nineveh has many people who are entrapped in their sinful lifestyles and don't know how to get out, who "cannot tell their right hand from their left" (v. 11). Jonah cared about the plant. Shouldn't God care about the city of Nineveh?

The phrase ("cannot tell their right hand from their left") has received much ink in attempts to explain its idiomatic meaning. Some have assumed it refers to young children who cannot tell the difference between their right hand and left hand. The Hebrew idiom, however, is the key to understanding the meaning. The idiom used here (*yada' ben . . . le*) occurs in only a few places in the Old Testament and means "to distinguish or discriminate between certain things."[16] For example, it is used in the book of 2 Samuel to describe the eighty-year-old priest, Barzillai, who protests that he is no longer able to taste the food and the wine for King David in order to discriminate between good and bad (see 2 Sam. 19:35). It is also used in Ezekiel a couple of times to describe one of the tasks given to the priests: teaching the people to discriminate between the clean and the unclean (see Ezek. 22:26; 44:23).

Since the idiom means "to distinguish," in Jonah it seems to be indicating that Nineveh has many people who are entrapped in their sinful lifestyles and don't know how to get out. These pagan people are helpless in their inability to make serious ethical discriminations. Surely they are not morally innocent—that's indicated by their own confession in chapter 3, not to mention the many other places in Scripture that allude to them as wicked and guilty—but they are helpless in the sense that they are trapped in their sins and undiscerning about how to escape them.

God highlights the superficiality of Jonah's ties to this plant. This is only a single plant and a lifeless one at that. Jonah has no claim to the plant whatsoever. Jonah has no claims before the bar of justice. All his appeals about God's dealings with the plant and with the Ninevites are out of court!

Jonah had set himself up as judge. He blurred the distinction between the creature and the Creator. He arrogated to himself the position of arbitrator of life and death from the humble stance of a sinful human creature. He had not acted in accordance with his station in life. He did not really know before whom he stood. A savage torpor had clouded his mind. A caustic sclerosis had covered his heart. Jonah was looking on the situation with unseeing eyes.

God has a right to do with Nineveh as he pleases. God has a right, as Creator, to do as he pleases with the plant. In verse 11 God directs his third question at Jonah—the whole book has been building toward this very moment: "Should I not be concerned about that great city?" This is much better translated, "May I not be concerned . . . ?"

What I wish to focus on here is the verb which the NIV translates in context as "should I not be concerned" (*'ahus*). With reference to the actions of a sovereign (for example, a ruler in instances of war or the administration of justice), this verb often denotes the power to spare or not spare a given individual. That is to say, "It relates to superiors who are [or are not] moved to pity toward those who are within their jurisdiction."[17]

Jonah had no right even over the plant. God had every right to exercise pity—over the plant, the city, the people of Nineveh, and Jonah himself. Nothing falls outside of God's jurisdiction. A similar sentiment was echoed by the apostle Paul many years later: "What then shall we say? Is God unjust? Not at all! For he says to Moses, 'I will have mercy on whom I have mercy, and I will have compassion on whom I have compassion.' It does not, therefore, depend on man's desire or effort, but on God's mercy" (Rom. 9:14–16). Jonah must recognize the absolute sovereignty and freedom of God to act as he pleases.

But the use of the verb *hus* is more significant than even this. It has to do not only with the rights of the Creator over the creature, but also with the *way* in which his sovereign privileges are carried out. For here in Jonah 4 *hus* is suffering action, "action executed with tears in the eyes."[18]

We see, then, that God's line of attack against Jonah's position is not against a narrow nationalism and ethnocentrism that developed among postexilic Jews (as is often thought). Rather the line of argumentation is "theologically grounded in the nature of God as Creator."[19] Douglas Stuart poignantly comments regarding Jonah 4:2: " 'What is God really like?' is thus a more important question in this book than the question 'What was Jonah really like?' "[20]

Could it be that God was using this story, a story originally written by a Jew to other Jews, in order to pose to Israel a depersonalized narrative, so that each one reading would answer the question for himself or herself? As Peter Craigie says: "In the tradition of the audience to whom the story was first told, everything suggested the answer 'No!' An evil gentile city should not experience the divine pity. But to say 'No' after hearing the story of Jonah would be embarrassing, not to say petty."[21]

The question leaves the reader engaged, unable to be aloof. This masterful short story ends in a way that entails application. As Janet Gaines says, "It is primarily the reader on whom God's final words land, the reader who is left to ponder their meaning, the reader who must decide what action to take next."[22] But how many biblical books end with a question in which God gets the last word? Interestingly, this book and the book of Nahum are the only two biblical books to end with a question. Both books concern the city of Nineveh. The book of Jonah ends on a note of compassion toward the city, but the book of Nahum ends on a note of judgment.[23]

What we see in the final chapter is God's pity not just on the weak and helpless but on the strong and the mighty. Those who have egregiously sinned are actually the objects of God's concern, care, and pity (both the Ninevites and Jonah). It is easy for us to pity the pitiable, but what about those who are not? This is what makes God's mercy so profound. Once we grasp this theological point, our own lives may be transformed so that we too are able to exercise pity. Most significant is the fact that a deep and profound understanding of God's amazing pity toward those who are obvious sinners may actually move us toward pity.

But this was not acceptable to Jonah. As George Landes states:

> He does not object to the divine compassion and salvation directed to those like himself, but when it is also effective for the wicked, he cannot abide it. Yet he is unwilling to live without his old belief; and because he refuses to let Yahweh transform his anger into love, his pity for plants into pity for people, his conception of what the object of the divine mercy ought to be into what Yahweh has shown him it actually is, he desperately longs to die.[24]

God is constant through the ages. In the New Testament, Christ was sincerely moved by compassion for his sheep and even those unwilling to become his sheep. A passage from the Gospels where Christ overlooks Jerusalem captures the profound compassion of the Savior: "O Jerusalem, Jerusalem, you who kill the prophets and stone those sent to you, how often I have longed to gather your children together, as a hen gathers her chicks under her wings, but you were not willing" (Matt. 23:37). Surely we may agree with the sentiment of John Murray that behind and within this lament there is something of the invitation from Matthew 11:28–30:[25] "Come to me, all you who are weary and burdened, and I will give you rest. Take my yoke upon you and learn from me, for I am gentle and humble in heart, and you will find rest for your souls. For my yoke is easy and my burden is light."

In the fullness of time, God has in Jesus Christ brought salvation to the nations, not just Israel. The compassion of God revealed so powerfully at the end of Jonah is quintessentially manifested on the hill of Golgotha. All of this foreshadowing in Jonah comes into sharper focus in what God has done in and through Jesus Christ for his own sheep. Truly, "Salvation comes from the LORD" (2:9).

Did Jonah eventually take to heart the lessons learned from this counseling session, which was in the form of a debate with God? The text does not say. The annals of history are silent. The Scriptures are silent. In some respects the point is moot because the questions are put to the current reader as well as to Jonah and Israel of old.

## FOR FURTHER REFLECTION

1. Commentators often compare Jonah with Elijah. Read 1 Kings 19 and contrast the behavior of Jonah with Elijah. What are the similarities and what are the differences?
2. What are the various ways in which God instructs and guides Jonah in chapter 4?
3. What do you think the ultimate message of chapter 4 is?

4. What are the three questions God asks of Jonah, and what is the significance of each?
5. In what ways can we individually identify with Jonah? How does the church as a whole identify with Jonah?
6. Will God's mercy transform your heart and remold your thinking?

# POSTSCRIPT

"Preachers who ignore the history of redemption in their preaching are ignoring the witness of the Holy Spirit to Jesus in all the Scriptures."[1] In our study of this short but profound little book of Jonah we have seen that it constantly points us forward to the "One who is greater than Jonah." In the church, our culture, and the academic world, however, there are many pressures against a responsible Christocentric reading of Jonah and the rest of the Old Testament.

The church has always affirmed appropriate application of the Holy Scriptures. This affirmation will obviously mean different things in regard to different parts of Scripture. Nevertheless, in the church presently there is much confusion over the issue of the proper application of preaching. Some have sounded an alarm against redemptive-historical preaching that is Christocentric and have even cast doubt on the usefulness of Reformed luminaries from the past such as Geerhardus Vos.

When preaching on Old Testament passages (I hope your minister does!), ministers should be taking pains to persuade people of responsible Christ-centered interpretations of the Old Testament. As Edmund Clowney has said, "Preaching Christ from the Old Testament means that we preach, not synagogue sermons, but sermons that take account of the full drama of redemption, and its realization in Christ."[2]

In academic circles, on the other hand, such a reading as the one that has been offered in this book might be caricatured as a Christian colonization of the Old Testament. The Old Testament, on the contrary, is not complete without the New, and therefore a Christocentric reading is not a "colonization" of the Old. Christ himself saw the book of Jonah as anticipating his own ministry and message, and therefore a redemptive-historical reading of Jonah is entirely appropriate for the postresurrection people of God.

There is another trend in Old Testament studies. The Old Testament, it is said, is made up of polyphonic voices from different times, different places, and different cultures. Thus there is no organic unity to the Scriptures, nor can there be. Now it is true that there are a myriad of different human voices embedded in different genres and emerging from different times and differing contexts. Indeed, these must be respected and assiduously studied and explained. Nevertheless, this does not supersede the facts that God is one and he has a well-orchestrated plan, which he executed throughout Old Testament and New Testament history. Privileged with hindsight, we can begin to observe the marvelous tapestry unfolding before our eyes. From our time in history we can see an all-wise God moving his creation forward to its climax, a redemptive-historical plan that not only marches forward but is acted upon from God's throne room in heaven.

Such an approach to preaching is not to take the Word of God away from the people of God; rather, it is to answer the question, "What is effective preaching?" Effective preaching is gospel proclamation from all of Scripture; it puts the spotlight where God delights to shine it: on the work of our Lord. Jesus Christ is the answer for our wounded hearts in this sin-cursed world. May God grant ministers the grace we need to obey our Lord's command, "Feed my sheep" (John 21:17).

# NOTES

## INTRODUCTION

1   Quoted in Thomas M. Bolin, *Freedom Beyond Forgiveness: The Book of Jonah Re-Examined* (Sheffield: Sheffield Academic Press, 1997), 13. The full history of the translation of the Latin letter is given there.

2   E. J. Young, *An Introduction to the Old Testament* (Grand Rapids: Eerdmans, 1965), 263.

3   R. T. France, *Jesus and the Old Testament: His Application of Old Testament Passages to Himself and His Mission* (Downers Grove, Ill.: InterVarsity, 1971), 78.

4   Yvonne Sherwood, *A Biblical Text and Its Afterlives: The Survival of Jonah in Western Culture* (Cambridge: Cambridge University Press, 2000), 14–15.

## CHAPTER ONE: ORIENTATION

1   Uriel Simon, *Jonah*, JPS Bible Commentary, ed. Nahum M. Sarna et al. (Philadelphia: Jewish Publication Society, 1999), xviii.

2   T. Desmond Alexander, *Jonah: An Introduction and Commentary* (Downers Grove, Ill.: InterVarsity, 1988), 91.

3   Karin Almbladh, *Studies in the Book of Jonah*, Acta Universitatis Upsaliensis: Studia Semitica Upsaliensia 7 (Uppsala: Almquist & Wiksell, 1986), 41.

4   "The Black Obelisk of Shalmaneser III," in *Ancient Near Eastern Texts Relating to the Old Testament*, ed. James B. Pritchard, 3d ed. (Princeton: Princeton University Press, 1969), 280.

5   Edmund P. Clowney, *Preaching and Biblical Theology* (Phillipsburg, N.J.: Presbyterian and Reformed, 1961), 92. Much of the survey

which follows in this chapter is a summary of Clowney's fine discussion of the introductory background of Jonah (pp. 92–98). Additionally, I have included some helpful ideas from the Jewish historian Yehezkel Kaufmann, *The Religion of Israel* (Chicago: University of Chicago Press, 1960), 128–29 and 273–90. Kaufmann was convinced of the absolute uniqueness of Israelite religion. He is helpful at some points but overstates his case at times also (for example, his insistence on the early composition of the book of Jonah).

6   Meredith G. Kline, *Kingdom Prologue: Genesis Foundations for a Covenantal Worldview* (Overland Park, Kans.: Two Age Press, 2000), 1–7.

7   Clowney, *Preaching*, 92–93.

8   Rosemary Nixon, *The Message of Jonah* (Downers Grove, Ill.: InterVarsity, 2003), 101.

9   Peter C. Craigie, *Twelve Prophets*, 2 vols. (Philadelphia: Westminster, 1984), 1:233.

10  See Moshe Held, "A Faithful Lover in an Old Babylonian Dialogue," *Journal of Cuneiform Studies* 15 (1961): 11–12; and Moshe Greenberg, "Hebrew *segulla* and Akkadian *sikiltu*," *Journal of the American Oriental Society* 71 (1951): 172–74.

11  Greenburg, "Hebrew *segulla*," 174.

12  Kaufmann, *Religion of Israel*, 128.

13  The love of Jonah for his own people motivating his reluctance to extend mercy to potential enemies of Israel is a traditional Jewish interpretation stretching back to Midrashic sources. See Louis Ginzberg, *The Legends of the Jews*, vol. 6 (Philadelphia: Jewish Publication Society, 1928), 349 n. 27.

14  Elie Wiesel, *Five Biblical Portraits* (Notre Dame: University of Notre Dame Press, 1981), 154.

CHAPTER TWO: THE RUNAWAY PROPHET (1:1–3)

1   Elie Wiesel, *Five Biblical Portraits* (Notre Dame: University of Notre Dame Press, 1981), 138–39.

2   See, for example, J. H. Stek, "The Message of the Book of Jonah," *Calvin Theological Journal* 4 (1969): 23–50.

3   Ibid., 38–40.

4  Edmund P. Clowney, *Preaching and Biblical Theology* (Phillipsburg, N.J.: Presbyterian and Reformed, 1961), 98.

5  Klaas Spronk, *Nahum* (Kampen: Kok Pharos, 1997), 20.

6  Ibid., 17.

7  Abraham Kuyper, *In the Shadow of Death: Meditations for the Sick-Room and at the Sick-Bed*, trans. John Hendrik De Vries (Audubon, N.J.: Old Paths Publications, 1994), 119.

## CHAPTER THREE: PANDEMONIUM ABOARD THE SHIP (1:4–6)

1  Jack M. Sasson, *Jonah*, Anchor Bible 24B (New York: Doubleday, 1990), 96–97.

2  Yvonne Sherwood, *A Biblical Text and Its Afterlives* (Cambridge: Cambridge University Press, 2000), 251.

3  Jacques Ellul, *The Judgment of Jonah*, trans. Geoffrey W. Bromiley (Grand Rapids: Eerdmans, 1971), 37.

## CHAPTER FOUR: PROPHET OVERBOARD (1:7–16)

1  For a clear introduction to this feature, see Tremper Longman III, *How to Read the Psalms* (Downers Grove, Ill.: InterVarsity, 1988), 101–4.

2  Jonathan Magonet, *Form and Meaning: Studies in Literary Techniques in the Book of Jonah* (Sheffield: Almond, 1983), 30–31.

3  This is different from the philosophical and ethical issue of whether God ever leaves us in situations where there is no righteous choice. That issue, a very important one theologically, is not under discussion here.

4  Thomas M. Bolin, *Freedom Beyond Forgiveness: The Book of Jonah Re-Examined* (Sheffield: Sheffield Academic Press, 1997), 88–90. Jack M. Sasson, *Jonah*, Anchor Bible 24B (New York: Doubleday, 1990), makes similar comments, but I am especially indebted to Bolin's insights into these passages and their application to this part of Jonah.

5  Sasson, *Jonah*, 142.

6  Yvonne Sherwood, *A Biblical Text and Its Afterlives* (Cambridge: Cambridge University Press, 2000), 246.

7   Hugh Martin, *The Prophet Jonah: His Character and Mission to Nineveh* (London: Banner of Truth Trust, 1958), 178–79.

8   Edmund P. Clowney, *The Unfolding Mystery: Discovering Christ in the Old Testament* (Colorado Springs: NavPress, 1988), 187.

9   Ibid.

10  Sasson, *Jonah*, 124–25.

11  Leslie Allen, *The Books of Joel, Obadiah, Jonah and Micah* (Grand Rapids: Eerdmans, 1976), 211.

12  André Lacocque and Pierre-Emmanuel Lacocque, *Jonah: A Psycho-Religious Approach to the Prophet* (Columbia, S.C.: University of South Carolina Press, 1990), 89.

13  Ellul, *The Judgment of Jonah*, trans. Geoffrey W. Bromiley (Grand Rapids: Eerdmans, 1971), 36–37.

CHAPTER FIVE: INTO THE FISH'S BELLY (1:17)

1   Rosemary Nixon, *The Message of Jonah* (Downers Grove, Ill.: InterVarsity, 2003), 127–8.

2   Terence E. Fretheim, *The Message of Jonah: A Theological Commentary* (Minneapolis: Augsburg, 1977), 93.

3   Jack M. Sasson, *Jonah*, Anchor Bible 24B (New York: Doubleday, 1990), 149.

4   Ibid.

5   Neil B. MacDonald (quoting James Barr), "The Philosophy of Language and the Renewal of Biblical Hermeneutics," in *Renewing Biblical Interpretation* (Grand Rapids: Zondervan, 2000), 123–24.

6   Horace D. Hummel, "The Old Testament Basis of Typological Interpretation," *Biblical Research* 9 (1964): 38–50.

7   For a brief and clear summary of the history of interpretation touching on these issues, Kevin Vanhoozer's book, *Is There a Meaning in This Text?* (Grand Rapids: Zondervan, 1998), 112–20, is commended to the reader (especially pastors).

8   Ibid., 119.

9   See Yvonne Sherwood, *A Biblical Text and Its Afterlives* (Cambridge: Cambridge University Press, 2000), 254ff.

10  For a detailed discussion, the reader may turn to R. T. France, *Jesus and the Old Testament* (Downers Grove, Ill.: InterVarsity, 1971), 80–82.

11 The author acknowledges that much of the analysis that follows is indebted to the fine discussion in ibid., 43ff.

12 R. T. France, *Matthew: Evangelist and Teacher* (Grand Rapids: Zondervan, 1989), 189.

13 Ibid., 189–90.

14 France, *Jesus and the Old Testament*, 75–76.

15 Sasson, *Jonah*, 157.

16 Joyce Baldwin, "Jonah," in *The Minor Prophets: An Exegetical and Expository Commentary*, ed. Thomas Edward McComiskey (Grand Rapids: Baker, 1993), 2:548.

CHAPTER SIX: PRAYER FROM THE DEPTHS:
PART ONE (2:1–6A)

1 George M. Landes, "The Kerygma of the Book of Jonah," *Interpretation* 21 (1967): 3–31.

2 Alastair Hunter, "Jonah from the Whale: Exodus Motifs in Jonah 2," in *The Elusive Prophet*, ed. J. C. deMoor (Leiden: Brill, 2001), 142–58.

3 Uriel Simon, *Jonah*, JPS Bible Commentary, ed. Nahum M. Sarna et al. (Philadelphia: Jewish Publication Society, 1999), 17ff.

4 For a technical discussion, the reader is referred to Frank Moore Cross, "The Prosody of Lamentations 1 and the Psalm of Jonah," in *From Epic to Canon: History and Literature in Ancient Israel* (Baltimore: Johns Hopkins University Press, 1998).

5 Cross, "Prosody," 133.

6 John R. Miles, "Laughing at the Bible: Jonah as Parody," in *On Humour and the Comic in the Hebrew Bible*, ed. Yehuda T. Radday and Athalya Brenner (Sheffield: Almond, 1990), 209. Terence E. Fretheim, *The Message of Jonah* (Minneapolis: Augsburg, 1977), 99, sees the quantity of references to the sea as almost double that of any other psalm.

7 Jack M. Sasson, *Jonah*, Anchor Bible 24B (New York: Doubleday, 1990), 172.

8 For an introduction to the subject, see Philip S. Johnston, *Shades of Sheol: Death and Afterlife in the Old Testament* (Downers Grove, Ill.: InterVarsity, 2002). My discussion follows many of Johnston's conclusions, especially on 71–85.

9  Johnston, *Shades of Sheol*, 75. Readers familiar with Geerhardus Vos will recognize that Vos had anticipated such a notion: "What they [the psalmists] feared was not death as such, nor that they might lose themselves in death, but that they might lose contact with Jehovah. . . . To lose touch with Him in Sheol would be painful, to miss Him at his final epiphany intolerable; it would be the supreme tragedy of religion. This is convincing proof that the eschatology of the Psalter seeks and loves nought above Jehovah Himself" ("Eschatology of the Psalter," in *The Pauline Eschatology* [Phillipsburg, N.J.: Presbyterian and Reformed, 1979], 346).

10  Much of the following discussion follows the contours of Klaas Schilder's discussion in *Christ Crucified* (Grand Rapids: Baker, 1940), 393–423.

11  Ibid., 402–5.

12  Ibid., 404–5.

13  See Vos, "Eschatology of the Psalter," 347.

## CHAPTER SEVEN: PRAYER FROM THE DEPTHS: PART TWO (2:6B–9)

1  Tikva Simone Frymer-Kensky, "The Judicial Ordeal in the Ancient Near East" (Ph.D. diss., Yale University, 1977), 1.

2  P. Kyle McCarter, "The River Ordeal in Israelite Literature," *Harvard Theological Review* 66 (1973): 403.

3  Ibid., 412.

4  See, for example, McCarter and also Alastair Hunter, "Jonah from the Whale," in *The Elusive Prophet*, ed. J. C. de Moor (Leiden: Brill, 2001), 142–58.

5  Jack M. Sasson, *Jonah*, Anchor Bible 24B (New York: Doubleday, 1990), 185, notes the curious reversal in the sequences of the imagery. More assertively, see the arguments by Hunter, "Jonah from the Whale," and Meredith G. Kline, *By Oath Consigned: A Reinterpretation of the Covenant Signs of Circumcision and Baptism* (Grand Rapids: Eerdmans, 1968), 50–52.

6  See Kline, *By Oath Consigned*, 60–62.

7  Ibid., 60.

8  Sasson, *Jonah*, 182.

9  Ibid., 183.

10  Ibid., 198.

11  John Calvin, *Commentaries on the Twelve Minor Prophets*, trans. John Owen, vol. 3, *Jonah, Micah, Nahum* (Edinburgh: Calvin Translation Society, 1847), 88.

12  Sasson, *Jonah*, 200.

13  See George M. Landes, "The Kerygma of the Book of Jonah," *Interpretation* 21 (1967): 16.

CHAPTER EIGHT: LESSONS ON REPENTANCE (2:10–3:10)

1  Yvonne Sherwood, *A Biblical Text and Its Afterlives* (Cambridge: Cambridge University Press, 2000), 259.

2  Jack M. Sasson, *Jonah*, Anchor Bible 24B (New York: Doubleday, 1990), 229.

3  David Marcus, "Nineveh's 'Three Days' Walk' (Jonah 3:3): Another Interpretation," in *On the Way to Nineveh: Studies in Honor of George Landes*, ed. Stephen L. Cook and S. C. Winter (Atlanta: Scholars, 1999), 42–53.

4  Ibid.

5  David Marcus (quoting D. F. Rauber), *From Balaam to Jonah: Anti-Prophetic Satire in the Hebrew Bible*, Brown Judaic Studies 301, ed. Ernest S. Frerichs, Shaye J. D. Cohen, and Calvin Godscheider (Atlanta: Scholars, 1995), 103.

6  See Kathleen Powers Erickson, *At Eternity's Gate: The Spiritual Vision of Vincent van Gogh* (Grand Rapids: Eerdmans, 1998).

7  George M. Landes, "The Kerygma of the Book of Jonah," *Interpretation* 21 (1967): 30.

8  Sherwood, *Biblical Text*, 260.

9  Kenneth M. Craig, *A Poetics of Jonah: Art in the Service of Ideology* (Columbia, S.C.: University of South Carolina Press, 1993), 53. Craig is stating a general principle and addressing his view of 4:5, not the text we are considering.

10  Clifford J. Collins, "From Literary Analysis to Theological Exposition: The Book of Jonah," *Journal of Translation and Textlinguistics* 7.1 (1995): 28-44.

11  See, e.g., Richard A. Muller, "Incarnation, Immutability, and the Case for Classical Theism," *Westminster Theological Journal* 45

(1983): 22–40. Muller demonstrates that the same kinds of questions were raised—and answered—in the ancient church.

12 Gregory A. Boyd, *God of the Possible* (Grand Rapids: Baker, 2000), 16.

13 Ibid.

14 Ibid., 14.

15 Ibid., 75.

16 Ibid., 85.

17 As a starting point, see Robert B. Strimple, "What Does God Know?" in *The Coming Evangelical Crisis*, ed. John H. Armstrong (Chicago: Moody, 1996), 139–54.

18 Michael S. Horton, *Covenant and Eschatology: The Divine Drama* (Louisville: Westminster John Knox, 2002), 8.

19 See especially Cornelius Van Til, *A Christian Theory of Knowledge* (Philadelphia: Presbyterian and Reformed, 1969), ch. 3.

20 John Calvin, *Institutes of the Christian Religion,* ed. John T. McNeill, 1.17.13.

## CHAPTER NINE: THE FINAL DEBATE (4:1–11)

1 See Uriel Simon, *Jonah*, JPS Bible Commentary, ed. Nahum M. Sarna et al. (Philadelphia: Jewish Publication Society, 1999), 36.

2 Here (at least with respect to the patterns of the use of the verb) I am following G. I. Davies, "The Uses of *R"* Qal and the Meaning of Jonah IV. 1," *Vetus Testamentum* 27 (1977): 105–11.

3 Jack M. Sasson, *Jonah*, Anchor Bible 24B (New York: Doubleday, 1990), 348–49.

4 Simon, *Jonah*, 36.

5 Ibid.

6 Simon points out that the attributes of justice are often left out of biblical prayer.

7 T. Desmond Alexander, *Jonah: An Introduction and Commentary* (Downers Grove, Ill.: InterVarsity, 1988), 127.

8 Simon, *Jonah*, 40.

9 John Calvin, *Commentaries on the Twelve Minor Prophets*, trans. John Owen, vol. 3, *Jonah, Micah, Nahum* (Edinburgh: Calvin Translation Society, 1847), 131.

10 Sasson, *Jonah*, 239.

11 Janet Howe Gaines, *Forgiveness in a Wounded World: Jonah's Dilemma* (Atlanta: Society of Biblical Literature, 1993), 106.

12  Ibid., 115.

13  Jacques Ellul, *The Judgment of Jonah*, trans. Geoffrey W. Bromiley (Grand Rapids: Eerdmans, 1975), 73–75.

14  See Aloysius Fitzgerald, *The Lord of the East Wind* (Washington, D.C.: The Catholic Biblical Association of America, 2002). Fitzgerald has thoroughly studied meteorological phenomena and relates them to many theophanic texts in the Hebrew Bible.

15  Calvin, *Jonah*, 130.

16  Hans Walter Wolff, *Obadiah and Jonah: A Commentary*, trans. Margaret Kohl (Minneapolis: Augsburg, 1986), 175. Also helpful on the use of the idiom is Donald Wiseman, "Jonah's Nineveh," *Tyndale Bulletin* 30 (1979): 29–51.

17  Terence E. Fretheim, "Jonah and Theodicy," *Zeitschrift für die alttestamentliche Wissenschaft* 90 (1978): 236.

18  Ibid. Also see Sheldon H. Blank, "Doest Thou Well to Be Angry? A Study in Self-Pity," *Hebrew Union College Annual* 26 (1955): 29–41.

19  Brevard S. Childs, *Introduction to the Old Testament as Scripture* (Philadelphia: Fortress, 1979), 427.

20  Douglas Stuart, *Hosea–Jonah*, Word Biblical Commentary (Waco: Word, 1987), 443.

21  Peter C. Craigie, *Twelve Prophets* (Philadelphia: Westminster, 1984), 1:20.

22  Gaines, *Forgiveness in a Wounded World*, 128.

23  See Tremper Longman III, "Nahum," in *The Minor Prophets: An Exegetical and Expository Commentary*, ed. Thomas Edward McComiskey (Grand Rapids: Baker, 1993), 2:829.

24  George M. Landes, "The Kerygma of the Book of Jonah," *Interpretation* 21 (1967): 29.

25  See John Murray, "The Free Offer of the Gospel," in *Collected Writings of John Murray* (Edinburgh: Banner of Truth Trust, 1982), 4:113–32.

## POSTSCRIPT

1  Edmund P. Clowney, *Preaching Christ in All of Scripture* (Wheaton, Ill.: Crossway, 2003), 10.

2  Ibid., 11.

# FOR FURTHER READING

The following sources were cited or referred to in the text.

Alexander, T. Desmond. *Jonah: An Introduction and Commentary.* Tyndale Old Testament Commentaries. Downers Grove, Ill.: InterVarsity, 1988.

Allen, Leslie. *The Books of Joel, Obadiah, Jonah and Micah.* New International Commentary on the Old Testament. Grand Rapids: Eerdmans, 1976.

Almbladh, Karin. *Studies in the Book of Jonah.* Acta Universitatis Upsaliensis: Studia Semitica Upsaliensia 7. Uppsala: Almquist & Wiksell, 1986.

Augustine. *On Christian Doctrine.* Translated with an introduction by D. W. Robertson Jr. New York: Liberal Arts, 1958.

Baldwin, Joyce. "Jonah." In *The Minor Prophets: An Exegetical and Expository Commentary*, edited by Thomas Edward McComiskey. Vol. 2. *Obadiah, Jonah, Micah, Nahum, and Habukkuk*, 543–90. Grand Rapids: Baker, 1993.

Blank, Sheldon H. "Doest Thou Well to Be Angry? A Study in Self-Pity." *Hebrew Union College Annual* 26 (1955): 29–41.

Bolin, Thomas M. *Freedom Beyond Forgiveness: The Book of Jonah Re-Examined.* Journal for the Study of the Old Testament Supplement Series 236. Sheffield: Sheffield Academic Press, 1997.

Boyd, Gregory A. *God of the Possible: A Biblical Introduction to the Open View of God.* Grand Rapids: Baker, 2000.

Calvin, John. *Commentaries on the Twelve Minor Prophets*. translated by John Owen. Vol. 3. *Jonah, Micah, Nahum*. Edinburgh: Calvin Translation Society, 1847.

Childs, Brevard S. *Introduction to the Old Testament as Scripture*. Philadelphia: Fortress, 1979.

Clowney, Edmund P. *Preaching and Biblical Theology*. Phillipsburg, N.J.: Presbyterian and Reformed, 1961.

———. *Preaching Christ in All of Scripture*. Wheaton, Ill.: Crossway, 2003.

———. *The Unfolding Mystery: Discovering Christ in the Old Testament*. Colorado Springs: NavPress, 1988.

Collins, Clifford John. "From Literary Analysis to Theological Exposition: The Book of Jonah." *Journal of Translation and Textlinguistics* 7.1 (1995): 28–44.

Craig, Kenneth M. *A Poetics of Jonah: Art in the Service of Ideology*. Columbia, S.C.: University of South Carolina Press, 1993.

Craigie, Peter C. *Twelve Prophets*. Daily Study Bible. Vol. 1. Philadelphia: Westminster, 1984.

Cross, Frank Moore. *From Epic to Canon: History and Literature in Ancient Israel*. Baltimore: Johns Hopkins University Press, 1998.

Davies, G. I. "The Uses of *R*" Qal and the Meaning of Jonah IV.1." *Vetus Testamentum* 27 (1977): 105–11.

Ellul, Jacques. *The Judgment of Jonah*. Translated by Geoffrey W. Bromiley. Grand Rapids: Eerdmans, 1971.

Erickson, Kathleen Powers. *At Eternity's Gate: The Spiritual Vision of Vincent van Gogh*. Grand Rapids: Eerdmans, 1998.

Fitzgerald, Aloysius. *The Lord of the East Wind*. Catholic Biblical Quarterly Monograph Series 34. Washington, D.C.: Catholic Biblical Association of America, 2002.

France, R. T. *Jesus and the Old Testament: His Application of Old Testament Passages to Himself and His Mission*. Downers Grove, Ill.: InterVarsity, 1971.

————. *Matthew: Evangelist and Teacher.* Grand Rapids: Zondervan, 1989.

Fretheim, Terence E. "Jonah and Theodicy." *Zeitschrift für die alttestamentliche Wissenschaft* 90 (1978): 227–37.

————. *The Message of Jonah: A Theological Commentary.* Minneapolis: Augsburg, 1977.

Frymer-Kensky, Tikva Simone. "The Judicial Ordeal in the Ancient Near East." Ph.D. diss., Yale University, 1977.

Gaines, Janet Howe. *Forgiveness in a Wounded World: Jonah's Dilemma.* Studies in Biblical Literature 5. Atlanta: Society of Biblical Literature, 1993.

Ginzberg, L. *The Legends of the Jews.* Vol. 6. Philadelphia: Jewish Publication Society, 1928.

Greenberg, Moshe. "Hebrew *segulla* and Akkadian *sikiltu.*" *Journal of the American Oriental Society* 71 (1951): 172–74.

Held, Moshe. "A Faithful Lover in an Old Babylonian Dialogue." *Journal of Cuneiform Studies* 15 (1961): 1–26.

Horton, Michael S. *Covenant and Eschatology: The Divine Drama.* Louisville: Westminster John Knox, 2002.

Hummel, Horace D. "The Old Testament Basis of Typological Interpretation." *Biblical Research* 9 (1964): 38–50.

Hunter, Alastair. "Jonah from the Whale: Exodus Motifs in Jonah 2." In *The Elusive Prophet: The Prophet as a Historical Person, Literary Character and Anonymous Artist,* edited by J. C. de Moor, 142–58. Oudtestamentische Studiën 45. Leiden: Brill, 2001.

Johnston, Philip S. *Shades of Sheol: Death and Afterlife in the Old Testament.* Downers Grove, Ill.: InterVarsity, 2002.

Kaufmann, Yehezkel. *The Religion of Israel.* Translated by Moshe Greenberg. Chicago: University of Chicago Press, 1960.

Kline, Meredith G. *By Oath Consigned: A Reinterpretation of the Covenant Signs of Circumcision and Baptism.* Grand Rapids: Eerdmans, 1968.

———. *Kingdom Prologue: Genesis Foundations for a Covenantal Worldview*. Overland Park, Kans.: Two Age Press, 2000.

Kuhrt, Amélie. *The Ancient Near East*. 2 vols. London: Routledge, 1995.

Kuyper, Abraham. *In the Shadow of Death: Meditations for the Sick-Room and at the Death-Bed*. Translated by John Hendrik De Vries. Audubon, N.J.: Old Paths Publications, 1994.

Lacocque, André, and Pierre-Emmanuel Lacocque. *Jonah: A Psycho-Religious Approach to the Prophet*. Columbia, S.C.: University of South Carolina Press, 1990.

Landes, George M. "The Kerygma of the Book of Jonah." *Interpretation* 21 (1967): 3–31.

Longman, Tremper, III. *How to Read the Psalms*. Downers Grove, Ill.: InterVarsity, 1988.

MacDonald, Neil B. "The Philosophy of Language and the Renewal of Biblical Hermeneutics." In *Renewing Biblical Interpretation,* edited by Craig Bartholomew, Colin Greene, and Karl Möller, 123–40. Scripture and Hermeneutics 1. Grand Rapids: Zondervan, 2000.

Magonet, Jonathan. *Form and Meaning: Studies in Literary Techniques in the Book of Jonah*. Bible and Literature Series 8. Sheffield: Almond, 1983.

Marcus, David. *From Balaam to Jonah: Anti-Prophetic Satire in the Hebrew Bible*. Atlanta: Scholars, 1995.

———. "Nineveh's 'Three Days' Walk' (Jonah 3:3): Another Interpretation." In *On the Way to Nineveh: Studies in Honor of George M. Landes*, edited by Stephen L. Cook and S. C. Winter, 42–53. ASOR Books 4. Atlanta: Scholars, 1999.

Marshall, I. Howard. "An Assessment of Recent Developments." In *It Is Written: Scripture Citing Scripture. Essays in Honour of Barnabas Lindars*, edited by D. A. Carson and H. G. M. Williamson, 1–21. Cambridge: Cambridge University Press, 1988.

Martin, Hugh. *The Prophet Jonah: His Character and Mission to Nineveh*. London: Banner of Truth Trust, 1958.

McCarter, P. Kyle. "The River Ordeal in Israelite Literature." *Harvard Theological Review* 66 (1973): 403–12.

Miles, John R. "Laughing at the Bible: Jonah as Parody." In *On Humour and the Comic in the Hebrew Bible*, edited by Yehuda T. Radday and Athalya Brenner, 203–15. Bible and Literature Series 23. Sheffield: Almond, 1990.

Muller, Richard A. "Incarnation, Immutability, and the Case for Classical Theism." *Westminster Theological Journal* 45 (1983): 22–40.

Murray, John. "The Free Offer of the Gospel." In *Collected Writings of John Murray*. Vol. 4, pp. 113–32. Edinburgh: Banner of Truth Trust, 1982.

Nixon, Rosemary. *The Message of Jonah*. Downers Grove, Ill.: InterVarsity, 2003.

Pritchard, James B., ed. *Ancient Near Eastern Texts Relating to the Old Testament*. 3d ed. Princeton: Princeton University Press, 1969.

Sasson, Jack M. *Jonah: A New Translation with Introduction, Commentary, and Interpretation*. Anchor Bible 24B. New York: Doubleday, 1990.

Schilder, Klaas. *Christ Crucified*. Translated by Henry Zylstra. Grand Rapids: Baker, 1940.

Sherwood, Yvonne. *A Biblical Text and Its Afterlives: The Survival of Jonah in Western Culture*. Cambridge: Cambridge University Press, 2000.

Simon, Uriel. *Jonah*. Translated by Lenn J. Schramm. The JPS Bible Commentary. Philadelphia: Jewish Publication Society, 1999.

Spronk, Klaas. *Nahum*. Historical Commentary on the Old Testament. Kampen: Kok Pharos, 1997.

Stek, J. H. "Biblical Typology Yesterday and Today." *Calvin Theological Journal* 5 (1970): 133–62.

————. "The Message of the Book of Jonah." *Calvin Theological Journal* 4 (1969): 23–50.

Strimple, Robert B. "What Does God Know?"In *The Coming Evangelical Crisis*, edited by John H. Armstrong, 139–54. Chicago: Moody, 1996.

Stuart, Douglas. *Hosea–Jonah.* Word Biblical Commentary. Waco, Tex.: Word, 1987.

Vanhoozer, Kevin J. *Is There a Meaning in This Text?* Grand Rapids: Zondervan, 1998.

Van Til, Cornelius. *A Christian Theory of Knowledge.* Philadelphia: Presbyterian and Reformed, 1969.

Vos, Geerhardus. "Eschatology of the Psalter." In *The Pauline Eschatology*, 323–65. Phillipsburg, N.J.: Presbyterian and Reformed, 1979.

Wenham, G. J. "The Coherence of the Flood Narrative." *Vetus Testamentum* 28 (1978): 336–48.

Wiesel, Elie. *Five Biblical Portraits.* Notre Dame: University of Notre Dame Press, 1981.

Wiseman, Donald J. "Jonah's Nineveh." *Tyndale Bulletin* 30 (1979): 29–51.

Wolff, Hans Walter. *Obadiah and Jonah: A Commentary.* Translated by Margaret Kohl. Minneapolis: Augsburg, 1986.

Young, E. J. *An Introduction to the Old Testament.* Grand Rapids: Eerdmans, 1965.

# INDEX OF SCRIPTURE